# Nuggets of Wisdom

## Quotes to Ponder and Inspire

Compiled by Brent N. Hunter

# Spirit Rising Productions

## (2013 Paperback Edition, 10/13/13)

ISBN: 978-0-9858821-8-1
Library of Congress Control Number: 2013911458
Edition: First

Spirit Rising Productions
2261 Market Street, Suite 637
San Francisco, CA 94114

Visit our website at www.SpiritRising.TV

Cover art by Mark Janssen (www.janssen-designs.com)

Printed in the United States of America

# Dedication

As an unknown wise person once said, "we do not inherit the earth from our ancestors, we borrow it from our children". This book is dedicated to children and people of young spirit, to whom we owe our best efforts at leaving the world better than we found it.

This book is also dedicated to my mother, Isçe Güner Gökcen Hunter, and father, Jack Nathan Hunter, who each helped make the world better in their own unique and special loving ways.

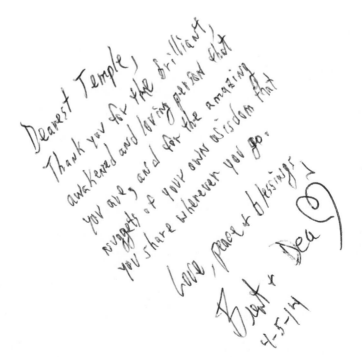

# Acknowledgements

Grateful acknowledgment is given to the sources of quotes in this book, all of whom have been identified to the greatest extent possible.

In addition, I want to thank my beloved Dea Shandera, who patiently provided loving and brilliant suggestions throughout the production of this book.

Finally, I want to thank my friend and colleague David Christel for his exceptional expertise with editing, page layout, formatting, quote source verification and for his eagle eye attention to detail.

# Table of Contents

# Introduction

We live in an infinite universe. It is imperative for us to recognize the importance of this concept, for it is the key to our future. It is irresponsible to be pessimistic in a field of infinite possibilities, and therefore, it is our responsibility to attempt to be positive in every situation in which we find ourselves. When we are guided by using the most inspiring and uplifting interpretation of any situation or experience, we will always be led towards the most positive outcome.

Let us be guided by our ideals, as we navigate the waters of life in the early 21st century. May this book of quotes remind us of our ideals, and may it help uplift and inspire us through these changing times.

During the course of posting a variety of inspiring and engaging quotes on social media for more than a decade, people have asked if I had all of the quotes available in a single place. *Nuggets of Wisdom* brings together many of the quotes I've collected over the years, as well as some of my own messages. If you would like to see these inspiring quotes and messages on a daily basis via social media, connect with me on Twitter at twitter.BrentHunter.TV, on Facebook at facebook.BrentHunter.TV, LinkedIn at linkedin.BrentHunter.TV, YouTube at youtube.BrentHunter.TV, Instagram at instagram.BrentHunter.TV and Pinterest at pinterest.BrentHunter.TV or at SpiritRising.TV .

I'm happy you've found this book and hope you'll carry these nuggets of wisdom close to your heart.

Enjoy!

Brent N. Hunter
August 13, 2013
West Hills, CA

# How to Use This Book

This book is not meant to be read as if it were a typical book. To make it easier to focus on and ponder each message to the fullest, there is only one quote on each page. Flip this book open to a "random" page and see what message appears, for it will be a synchronistic message from the universe. Feel free to leave the book open for the entire day so that you can ponder the message it contains for you (the spiral-bound edition is especially useful for this purpose). Daily use is recommended for the most powerful and sustained effect.

The infinity symbol at the bottom of the pages with quotes will remind you of your true nature as an infinite being living in an infinite cosmos.

"We are not physical beings
having a spiritual experience,
we are spiritual beings
having a human experience."

~ Teilhard de Chardin

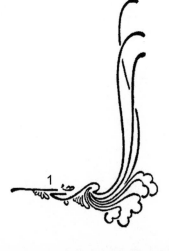

"'*Stay*' is a charming word
in a friend's vocabulary."

~ Louisa May Alcott

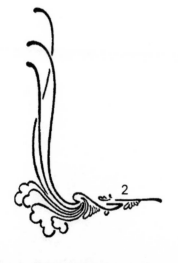

2

*"A business*
*that makes nothing but money*
*is a poor business."*

~ Henry Ford

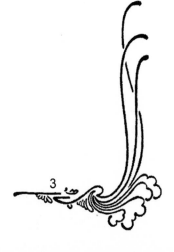

"*A candle loses nothing
by lighting another candle.*"

~ Proverb

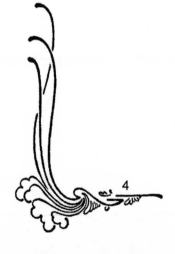

4

"*A cat's eyes are windows enabling us to see into another world.*"

~ Irish Legend

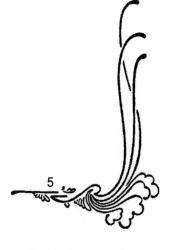

5

"*A fanatic is one*
*who can't change his mind*
*and won't change*
*the subject.*"

~ Sir Winston Churchill

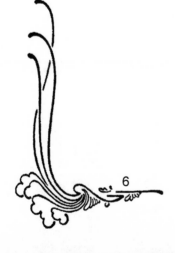

"A friend
is one before whom
I may think aloud."

~ Ralph Waldo Emerson

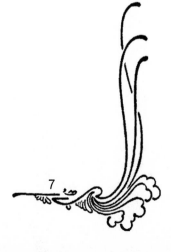

"*The inspiration you seek
is already within you.
Be silent and listen.*"

~ Jalāl ad-Dīn Muhammad Balkhī "Rumi"

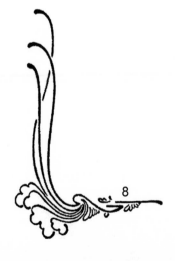

"*A friend knows
the song in my heart
and sings it to me
when memory fails.*"

~ Donna Roberts

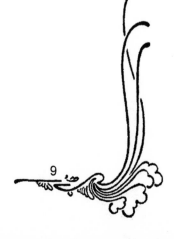

"*A good heart
is better than all the heads
in the world.*"

~ Edward Bulwer-Lytton

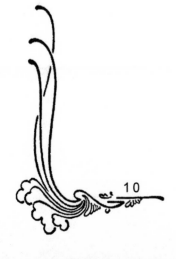

"*A hero is someone who understands the responsibility that comes with his or her freedom.*"

~ Bob Dylan

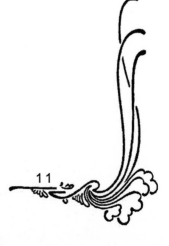

"*A house divided against itself cannot stand.*"

~ Abraham Lincoln

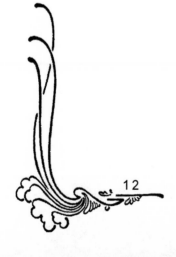

"*A journey of a thousand miles begins and ends with a single step.*"

~ Lao Tzu

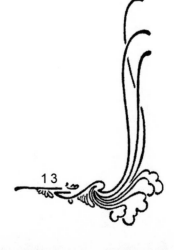

"*A kiss is a lovely trick
designed by nature
to stop speech when words
become superfluous.*"

~ Ingrid Bergman

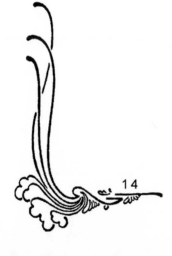

14

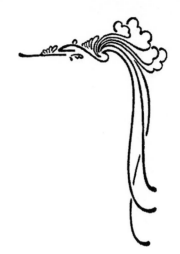

"*A man is but the product of his thoughts; what he thinks, he becomes.*"

~ Mahatma Gandhi

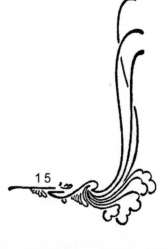

"*A man
never stands as tall
as when he kneels
to help a child.*"

~ Knights of Pythagoras

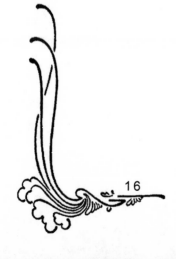

"*A one-word solution
to all the problems
the world is facing today
is 'compassion.'*"

~ Mātā Amṛtānandamayī Devī "Amma"

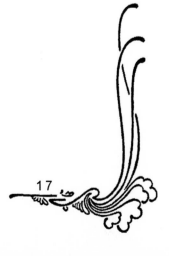

"*A paradox to ponder:*
*Everything you can imagine*
*is real and everything real*
*is an illusion.*"

~ Brent N. Hunter

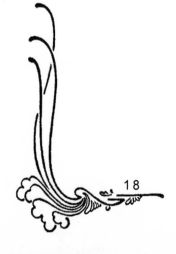

"*A pat on the back
is only a few vertebrae
removed from
a kick in the pants,
but is miles ahead
in results.*"

~ Ella Wheeler Wilcox

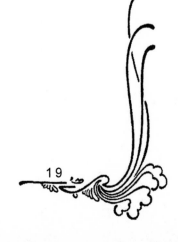

*"The purpose of conflict is to restore harmony."*

~ Brent N. Hunter

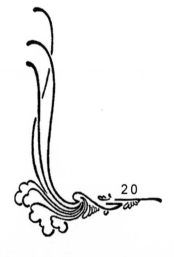

"Light up
the fire of love inside
and blaze the thoughts away."

~ Jalāl ad-Dīn Muhammad Balkhī "Rumi"

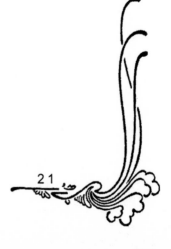

*"A person who wants
to lead the orchestra
must turn her or his back
on the crowd."*

~ Max Lucado

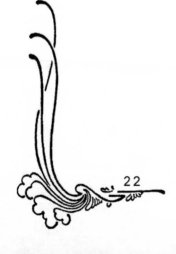

22

"*A rising tide
lifts all boats.*"

~ Proverb

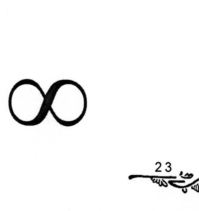

"A rock pile ceases to be
a rock pile the moment
a single man contemplates it,
bearing within him
the image of a cathedral."

~ Antoine de Saint-Exupery

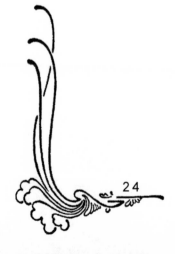

24

"A friend
is the one who comes in
when the whole world
has gone out."

~ Grace Pulpit

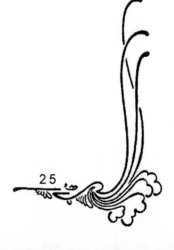

"*A ship in harbour is safe,
but that is not what ships
are built for.*"

~ William Shedd

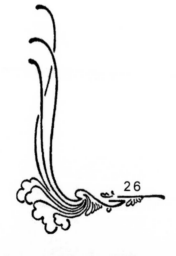

"*A smile is the beginning of peace.*"

~ Mother Teresa

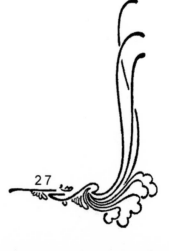

"*A teacher affects eternity;
he can never tell where
his influence stops.*"

~ Henry Brooks Adams

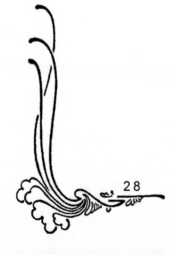

"The ultimate measure
of a person is not where
one stands in moments of
comfort and convenience,
but in times of challenge
and controversy."

~ Martin Luther King, Jr.

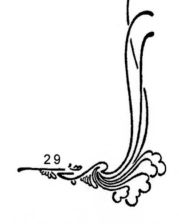

"A true friend
is one soul in two bodies."

~ Aristotle

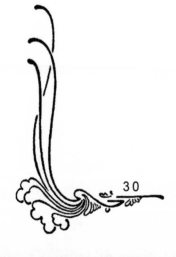

"*Act as if what you do
makes a difference.
It does.*"

~ William James

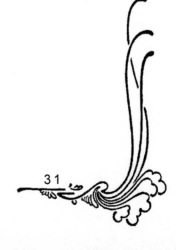

*"Adopt the pace of nature:
her secret is patience."*

~ Ralph Waldo Emerson

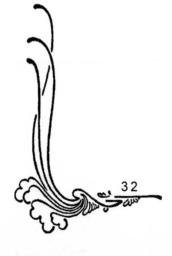

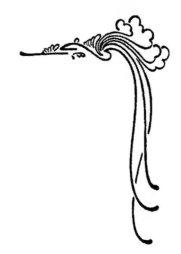

"*Respond to every call
that excites your spirit.*"

~ Jalāl ad-Dīn Muhammad Balkhī "Rumi"

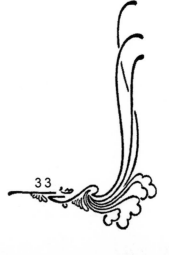

33

"*Aerodynamically
the bumblebee
shouldn't be able to fly,
but it doesn't know that
so it goes on flying anyway.*"

~ Mary Kay Ash

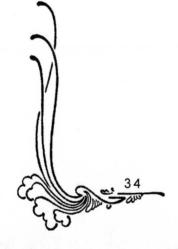

"After the game
is before the game."

~ Sepp Herberger

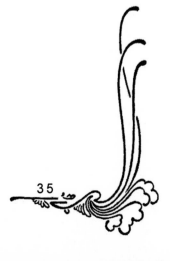

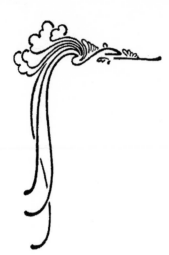

"After the game,
the king and the pawn
go into the same box."

~ Proverb

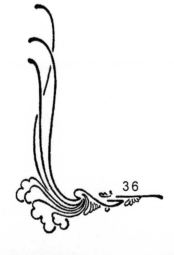

"There are two ways to live:
you can live
as if nothing is a miracle;
you can live as if everything
is a miracle."

~ Albert Einstein

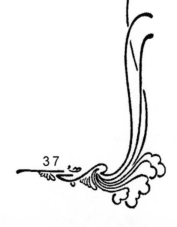

"*Age is an issue
of mind over matter.
If you don't mind,
it doesn't matter.*"

~ Mark Twain

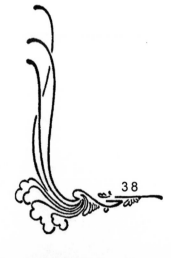

"*Aim above morality.*
*Be not simply good,*
*be good for something.*"

~ Henry David Thoreau

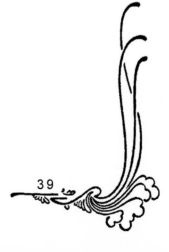

"All I can ask of myself
is to be the best
I can possibly be,
if I hit a wall
I plow through it."

~ Unknown

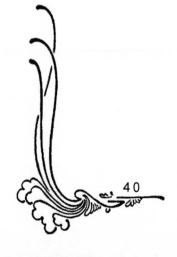

"*All of nature
is a canvas painted
by the hand of God.*"

~ Unknown

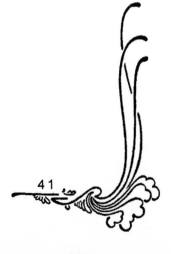

"*All serious daring
starts from within.*"

~ Harriet Beecher Stowe

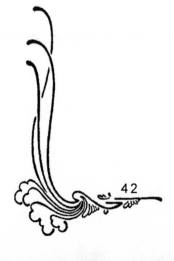

"All the world's a stage
and all the men and women
merely players:
they have their exits
and their entrances;
And one man in his time
plays many parts."

~ William Shakespeare

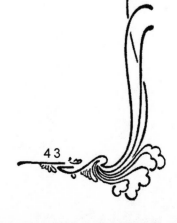

"*Love rests
on no foundation.
It is an endless ocean,
with no beginning or end.*"

~ Jalāl ad-Dīn Muhammad Balkhī "Rumi"

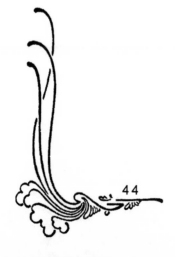

*"Alone we can do so little;*
*together we can do*
*so much."*

~ Helen Keller

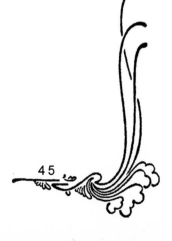

"*All achievements,
all earned riches,
have their beginning
in an idea.*"

~ Napoleon Hill

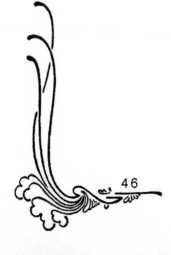

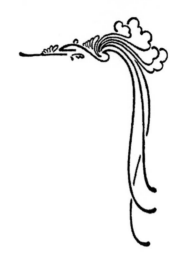

"*Always be
a first-rate version
of yourself instead of
a second-rate version
of someone else.*"

~ Judy Garland

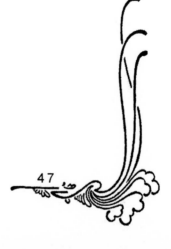

"*Always bear in mind
that your own resolution
to succeed is more important
than any other one thing.*"

~ Abraham Lincoln

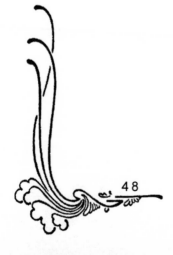

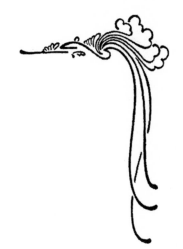

"Always give
without remembering,
and always receive
without forgetting."

~ Brian Tracy

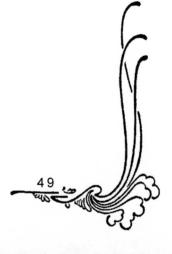

"Within your heart,
keep one still, secret spot
where dreams may go."

~ Louise Driscoll

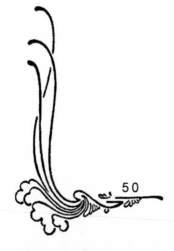

50

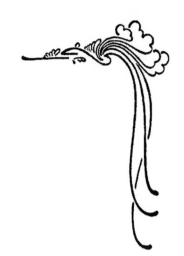

"*Always remember
that the future comes
one day at a time.*"

~ Dean Acheson

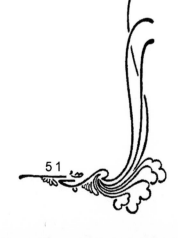

*"You don't have a life.*
*You ARE life."*

~ Eckhart Tolle

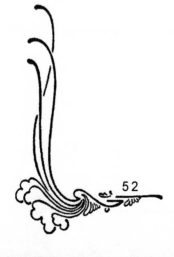

"Always seek out
the seed of triumph
in every adversity."

~ Og Mandino

53

"America
will never be destroyed
from the outside.
If we falter
and lose our freedoms,
it will be because
we destroyed ourselves."

~ Abraham Lincoln

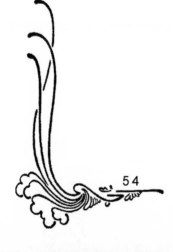

"In silence
there is eloquence.
Stop weaving and see how
the pattern improves."

~ Jalāl ad-Dīn Muhammad Balkhī "Rumi"

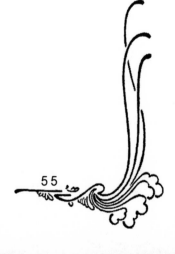

*"An affirmative thought
is 100 times more powerful
than a negative one."*

~ "The Secret" movie

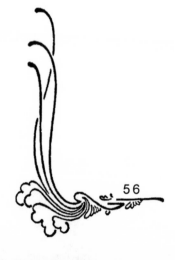

"*An enormous amount of energy becomes available once we give up the need to be right.*"

~ Deepak Chopra

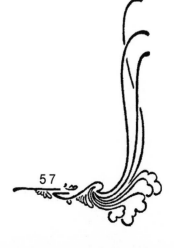

"*An eye for an eye
will make the whole world
blind.*"

~ Mahatma Gandhi

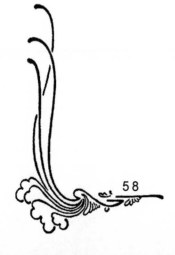

"*And when
the broken-hearted people
living in the world today agree,
there will be an answer,
Let It Be.*"

~ The Beatles

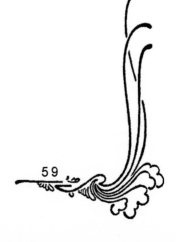

"And you?
When will you begin
that long journey
into yourself?"

~ Jalāl ad-Dīn Muhammad Balkhī "Rumi"

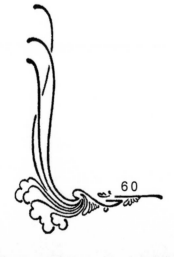

"*Any sufficiently advanced technology is indistinguishable from magic.*"

~ Arthur C. Clarke

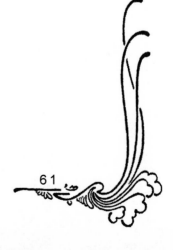

*"Anyone who has never
made a mistake
has never tried anything new."*

~ Albert Einstein

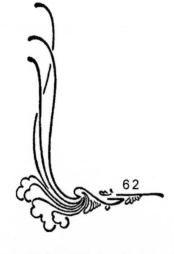

"*Anything in life worth having is worth working for.*"

~ Andrew Carnegie

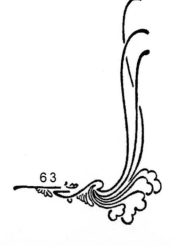

*"As for the future,*
*your task is not to foresee it,*
*but to enable it."*

~ Antoine de Saint-Exupery

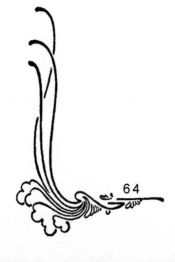

"*As we focus less
on what we're not
and more on all we are —
we'll step into more of
our bigness.*"

~ Unknown

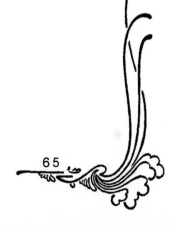

"At the center of your being
you have the answer;
you know who you are
and what you want."

~ Lao Tzu

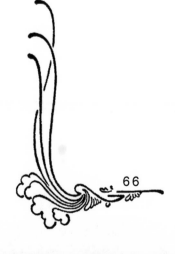

*"At the height of laughter,
the universe is flung into
a kaleidoscope of
new possibilities."*

~ Jean Houston

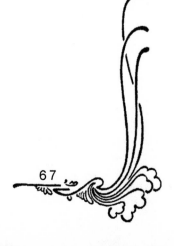

*"Autumn*
*is a second spring*
*where every leaf is a flower."*

~ Albert Camus

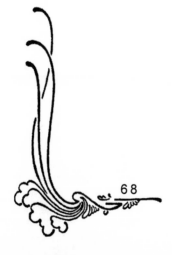

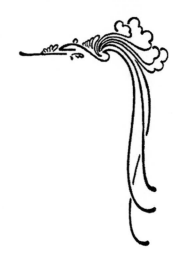

"*You must love in such a way that the person you love feels free.*"

~ Jalāl ad-Dīn Muhammad Balkhī "Rumi"

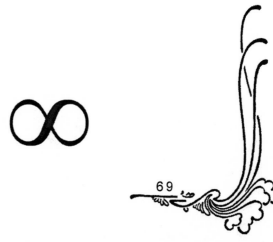

69

"*Life can only be
understood backwards;
but it must be lived forwards.*"

~ Søren Kierkegaard

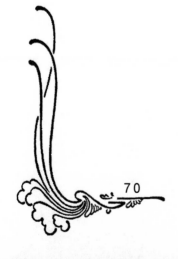

"Be a lamp or a lifeboat
or a ladder.
Help someone's soul heal.
Walk out of your house
like a shepherd."

~ Jalāl ad-Dīn Muhammad Balkhī "Rumi"

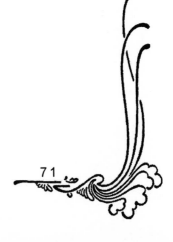

71

"*Be content to act,
and leave the talking to others.*"

~ Baltasar Gracián y Morales

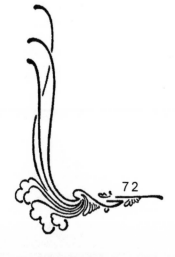

"The real measurement
of success is
who you're becoming
versus
what you are accumulating."

~ Robin Sharma

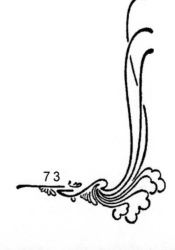

"Be kind whenever possible.
It is always possible."

~ HH The Dalai Lama

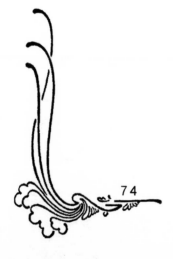

74

"Be like the flower,
turn your face to the sun."

~ Kahlil Gibran

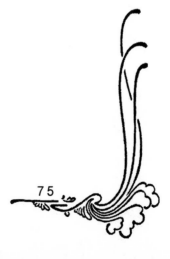

"Be miserable.
Or motivate yourself.
Whatever has to be done,
it is always your choice."

~ Wayne Dyer

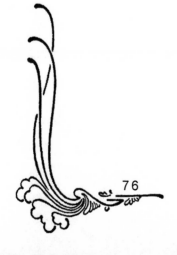

"Be more splendid,
more extraordinary.
Use every moment
to fill yourself up."

~ Oprah Winfrey

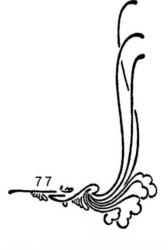

*"Be picky
about what you think."*

~ Unknown

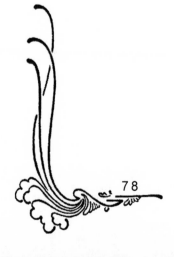

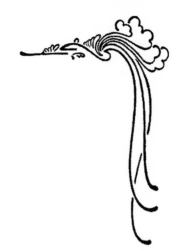

"*Be right, be wrong,
just BE.*"

~ Brent N. Hunter

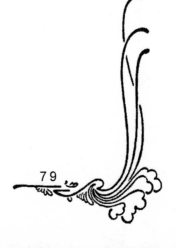

"Choose a job you love,
and you will never
have to work
a day in your life."

~ Confucius

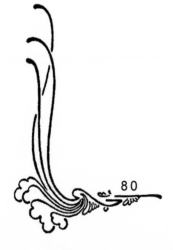

"Being nice to people
you don't get along with
isn't being two-faced,
it's being mature."

~ Brent N. Hunter

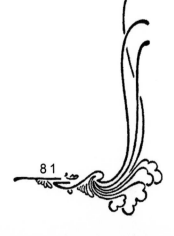

"Believe
and your belief
will actually create the fact."

~ William James

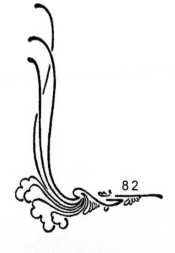

"*Better to do something imperfectly than to do nothing perfectly.*"

~ Robert H. Schuller

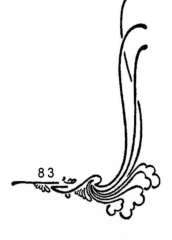

"Raise your words, not voice.
It is rain
that grows flowers,
not thunder."

~ Jalāl ad-Dīn Muhammad Balkhī "Rumi"

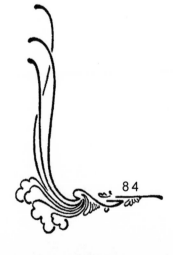

"*Birds sing after a storm;
why shouldn't people
feel as free to delight in
whatever remains to them?*"

~ Rose F. Kennedy

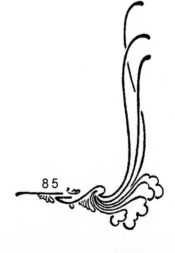

"*Breakdowns
can create breakthroughs.
Things fall apart
so things can fall together.*"

~ Anonymous

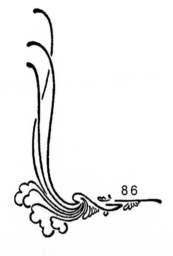

"*Bridges have two sides,*
*just like every story*
*has two sides.*
*We can come together*
*by meeting in the middle.*"

~ Brent N. Hunter

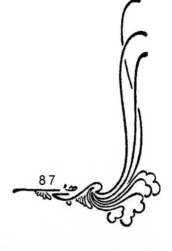

"*By prizing heartfulness
above faultlessness,

we may reap more

from our effort

because we're more likely

to be changed by it.*"

~ Sharon Salzberg

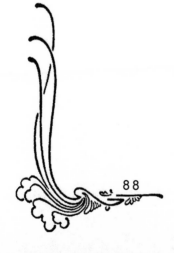

"Challenge is a dragon
with a gift in its mouth.
Tame the dragon
and the gift is yours."

~ Noela Evans

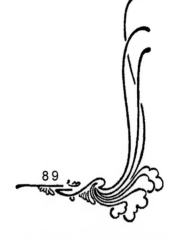

"Change your thoughts
and you change your world."

~ Norman Vincent Peale

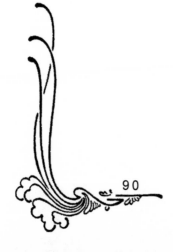

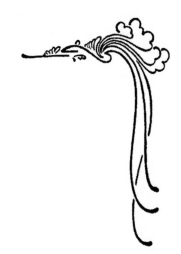

*"Being human*
*explains everything*
*but excuses nothing."*

~ Brent N. Hunter

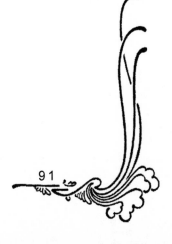

"*Each moment
contains a hundred messages
from God.*"

~ Jalāl ad-Dīn Muhammad Balkhī "Rumi"

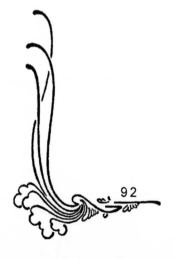

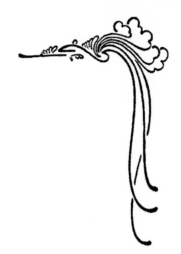

*"Compassion*
*is the basis of morality."*

~ Arthur Schopenhauer

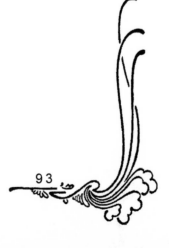

"Concentrated power
has always been
the enemy of liberty."

~ Ronald Reagan

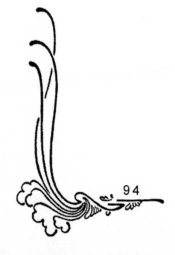

"Confidence is contagious.
So is lack of confidence."

~ Vince Lombardi

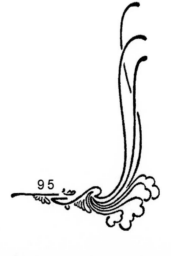

95

"Conflict
is a learning experience
when we are not aware
of our choices."

~ Unknown

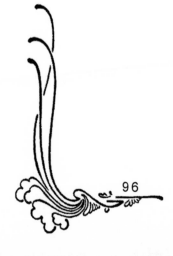

"Conscience is the inner voice
which warns us that
someone may be looking."

~ H.L. Mencken

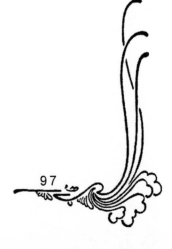

"There is one thing stronger
than all the armies
in the world, and that is,
an idea
whose time has come."

~ Victor Hugo

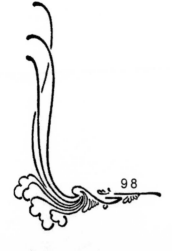

"Consider the rights of others
before your own feelings,
and the feelings of others
before your own rights."

~ John Wooden

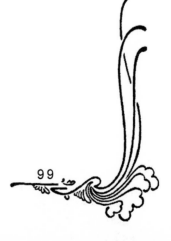

"Continuous improvement
is better than
delayed perfection."

~ Mark Twain

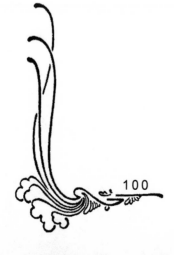

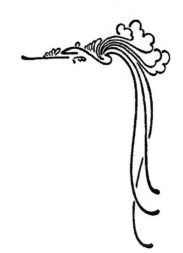

"*Courage*
*is being scared to death —*
*but saddling up anyway.*"

~ John Wayne

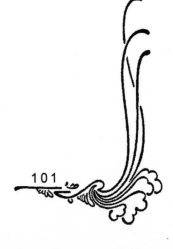

*"You are not
a drop in the ocean.
You are the entire ocean,
in a drop."*

~ Jalāl ad-Dīn Muhammad Balkhī "Rumi"

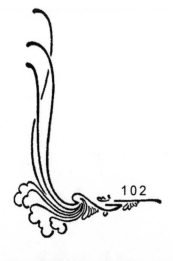

*"Courage is the power to let go of the familiar."*

~ Raymond Lindquist

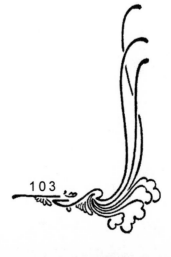

"Courage is what it takes
to stand up and speak.
Courage is also
what it takes
to sit down and listen."

~ Sir Winston Churchill

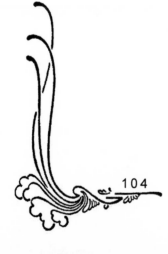

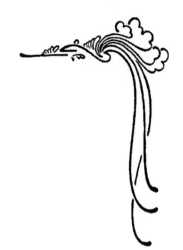

"Determine that the thing
can and shall be done,
and then we shall find
the way."

~ Abraham Lincoln

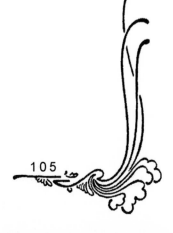

*"Discovery consists in seeing what everyone else has seen but understanding it for the first time."*

~ Albert Szent-Györgyi

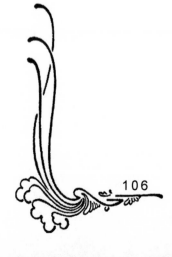

"Do not do unto others
what you would not like done
to yourself."

~ The Golden Rule

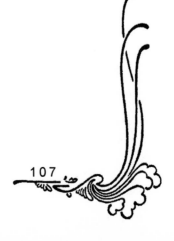

"Do not fear pressure,
for pressure
is what turns stones
into diamonds."

~ Unknown

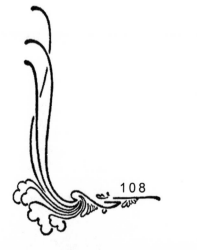

"Do not give thought
to that
which you do not want
— in thinking it
you are creating it."

~ Unknown

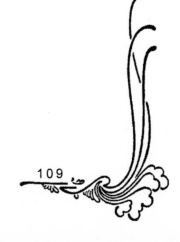

"Do not overrate
what you have received,
nor envy others.
He who envies others
does not obtain
peace of mind."

~ Buddha

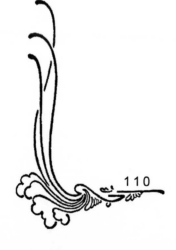

"Do not worry if you have
built your castles in the air.
They are where they should be.
Now put the foundations
under them."

~ Henry David Thoreau

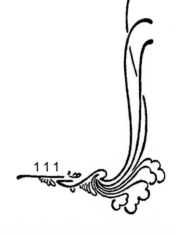

*"I belong to no religion.*
*My religion is Love.*
*Every heart is My temple."*

~ Jalāl ad-Dīn Muhammad Balkhī "Rumi"

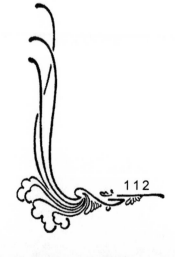

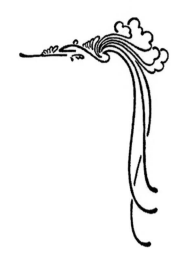

"Do what you can,
with what you have,
where you are."

~ Theodore Roosevelt

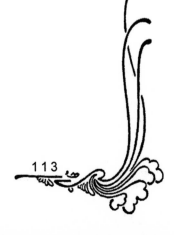

"Do you have a dream?
If not, create one.
Dreams are what keep us
going and inspired."

~ Brent N. Hunter

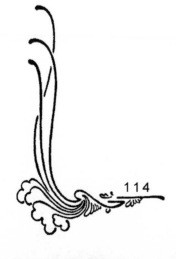

"Do you not feel
a thrill through the air
with notes of a song
from a distant shore?"

~ Deepak Chopra

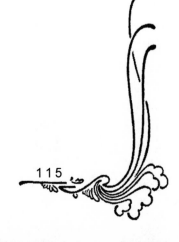

"Do, or do not.
There is no 'try.'"

~ Yoda

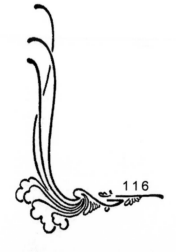

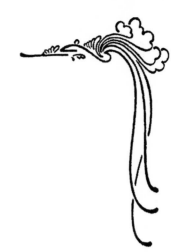

"Doing the best
at this moment
puts you in the best place
for the next moment."

~ Oprah Winfrey

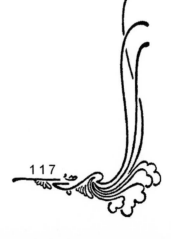

*"Don't ask 'why.'*
*Ask instead, 'why not?'"*

John F. Kennedy

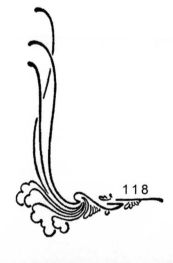

"Don't be distracted
by criticism.
The only taste of success
some people have is when they
take a bite out of you."

~ Zig Ziglar

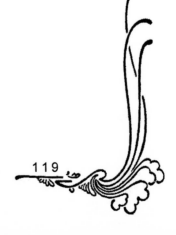

"Don't believe
everything you think."

~ Unknown

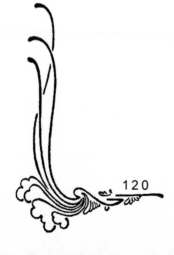

"Don't count every hour
in the day,
make every hour in the day
count."

~ Isak Dinesen

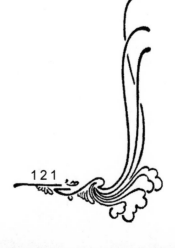

"Set your life on fire.
Seek those
who fan your flames."

~ Jalāl ad-Dīn Muhammad Balkhī "Rumi"

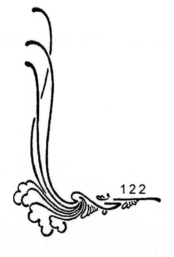

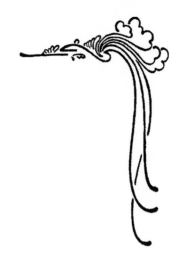

"Don't count the days,
make the days count."

~ Unknown

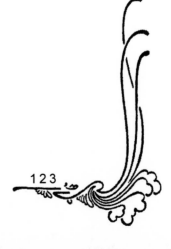

*"Don't curse the darkness —*
*light a candle."*

~ Chinese Proverb

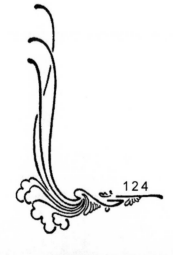

"Don't find fault,
find a remedy."

~ Henry Ford

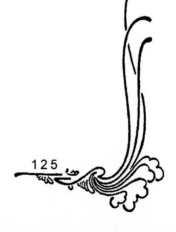

"Don't go into business
to get rich.
Do it to enrich people.
It will come back to you."

~ Stew Leonard

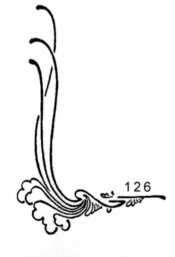

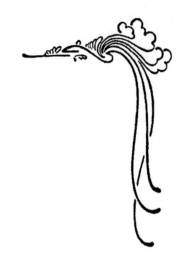

"Don't grow old saying,
'I wish I had.
I should have.
Why didn't I?'"

~ M. Shields

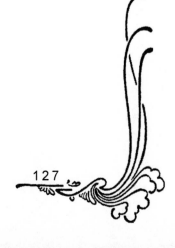

"Don't judge each day
by the harvest you reap,
but by the seeds you plant."

~ Robert Louis Stevenson

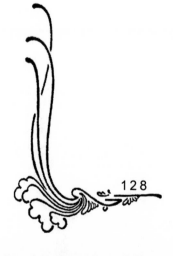

"Don't miss out
on a blessing
because it isn't packaged
the way you expect."

~ Anonymous

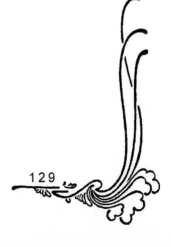

"*Dream lofty dreams,
and as you dream,
so shall you become.*"

~ James Allen

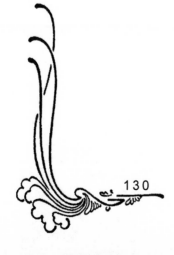

"*Let silence
take you to the core of life.*"

~ Jalāl ad-Dīn Muhammad Balkhī "Rumi"

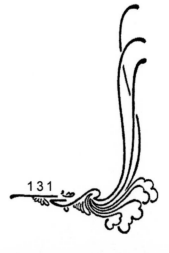

*"Drive thy business*
*or it will drive thee."*

~ Benjamin Franklin

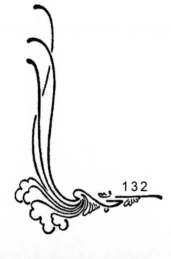

*"E Pluribus Unum*
*'Out of Many, One.'"*

~ Motto on the Seal of the United States

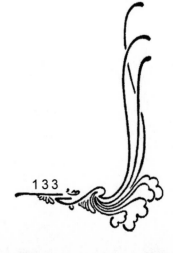

"Each breath connects us
to all life on the planet.
The same molecules cycle
thru all of us over time."

~ Stephen Dinan

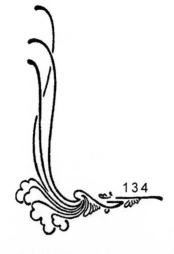

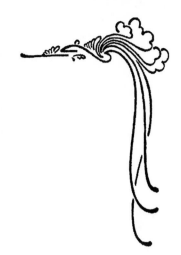

"Each friend represents
a world in us,
a world possibly not born
until they arrive."

~ Anaïs Nin

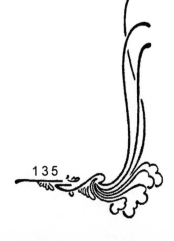

"*Education is what remains
after one has forgotten
what one has learned
in school.*"

~ Albert Einstein

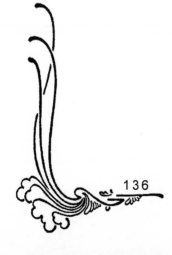

"Embrace all of the parts
of yourself: the good,
not-so-good and ugly,
accept these parts
and they will transform,
and you will be free."

~ Unknown

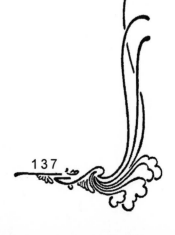

"*Enjoy the beauty of today,*
*wherever you are,*
*whoever you are*
*and whatever you do!!!*"

~ Brent N. Hunter

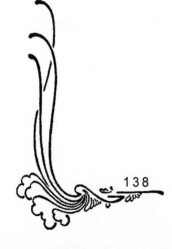

"*Eternity
is not endless duration.
It transcends and exists
outside time.
It is our real home.*"

~ Deepak Chopra

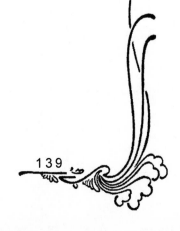

"*Every artist was first an amateur.*"

~ Ralph Waldo Emerson

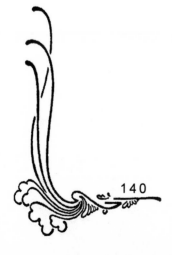

"What matters
is how quickly you do
what your soul wants!"

~ Jalāl ad-Dīn Muhammad Balkhī "Rumi"

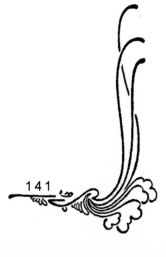

"*Every day
holds the possibility
of a miracle.*"

~ Elizabeth David

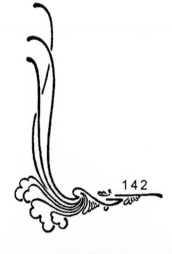

"They say that money
can't buy happiness,
but tell that to the 16,000
children around the world
who will starve to death
today."

~ Brent N. Hunter

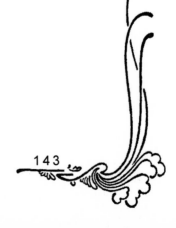

"*Every man must decide
whether he will walk in
the light of creative altruism
or darkness of
destructive selfishness.*"

~ Martin Luther King, Jr.

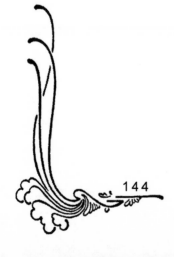

"*Every person you meet*
*opens the door to*
*a new world of possibilities.*
*Greet each morning with*
*the same reverence*
*and optimism.*"

~ Unknown

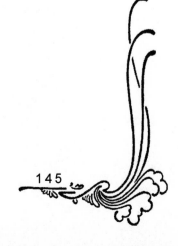

"Every problem has in it
the seeds of its own solution.
If you don't have
any problems,
you don't get any seeds."

~ Norman Vincent Peale

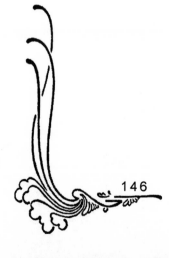

*"Every strike brings me closer to the next home run."*

~ Babe Ruth

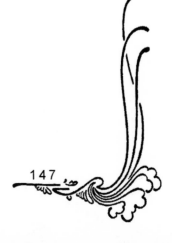

"*Everything comes to him who hustles while he waits.*"

~ Thomas Edison

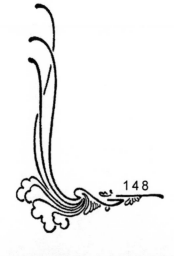

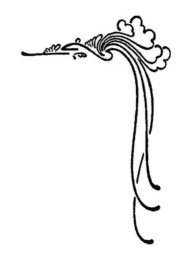

"Everything will be O.K
at the end.
If it's not O.K,
then it's not the end."

~ Unknown

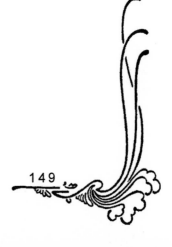

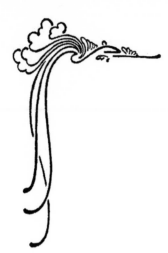

"*Everything you can imagine
is real.*"

~ Pablo Picasso

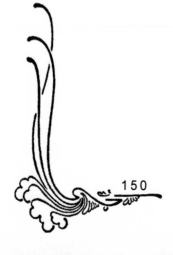

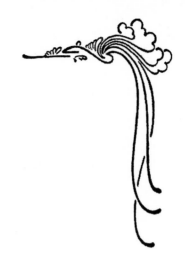

"*Excellence is doing
the right thing
even when nobody
is watching you.*"

~ Joel Osteen

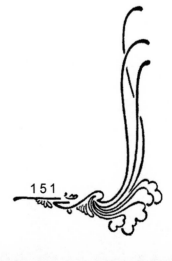

"*Whatever purifies you
is the right path.*"

~ Jalāl ad-Dīn Muhammad Balkhī "Rumi"

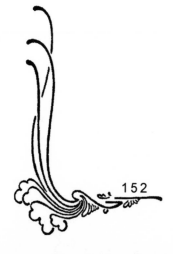

"Excellence
is to do a common thing
in an uncommon way."

~ Booker T. Washington

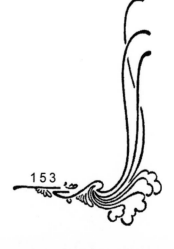

"*Faith consists in believing
when it is beyond the power
of reason to believe.*"

~ Voltaire

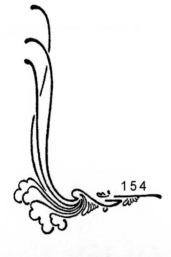

*"Fall seven times,
stand up eight."*

~ Japanese Proverb

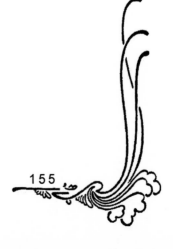

"Circumstances
do not make a man,
they reveal him."

~ Wayne Dyer

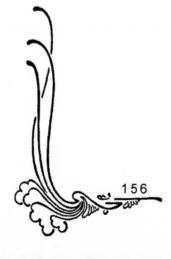

"Fear defeats more people
than any other one thing
in the world."

~ Ralph Waldo Emerson

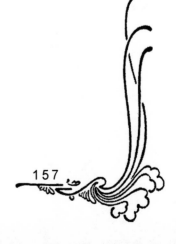

"*Beauty is eternity
gazing at itself in a mirror.*"

~ Kahlil Gibran

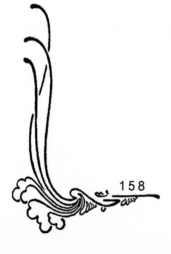

"Fear grows in darkness;
if you think there's
a bogeyman around,
turn on the light."

~ Dorothy Thompson

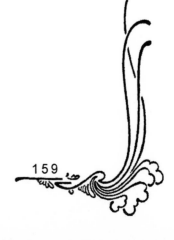

*"Fire cannot burn it,*
*water cannot wet it,*
*wind cannot dry it,*
*weapons cannot shatter it.*
*The soul is beyond time."*

~ Sai Baba Gita

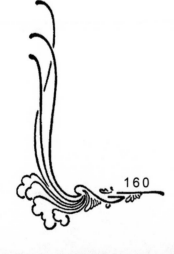

"First keep the peace
within yourself,
then you can also bring peace
to others."

~ Thomas à Kempis

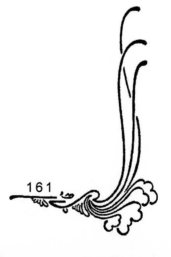

"The universe is uncaused,
like a net of jewels
in which each is
the reflection of the others
in a fantastic interrelated
harmony without end."

~ Ramesh Balsekar

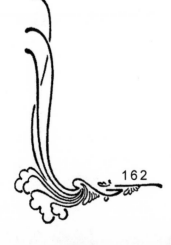

"First they ignore you.
Then they laugh at you.
Then they fight you.
Then you win."

~ Mahatma Gandhi

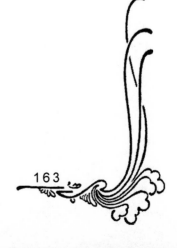

*"First you must learn
to play by the rules,
then you must forget the rules
and play from your heart."*

~ Unknown

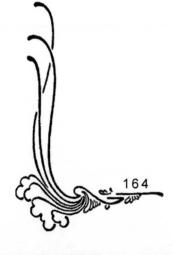

"*Hear the passage into silence
and be that.*"

~ Jalāl ad-Dīn Muhammad Balkhī "Rumi"

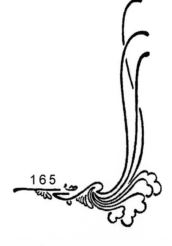

"Flaming enthusiasm,
backed up by horse sense
and persistence,
is the quality
that most frequently
makes for success."

~ Dale Carnegie

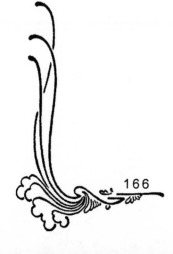

"Focus
on where you want to go,
not on what you fear."

~ Anthony Robbins

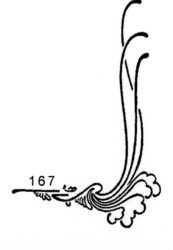

"*Follow your bliss.*"

~ Joseph Campbell

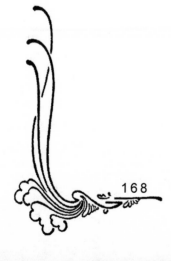

"For any
challenging situation,
ask what is the gift?
Why is this perfect?
You'll be amazed,
the answers always come!"

~ Brent N. Hunter

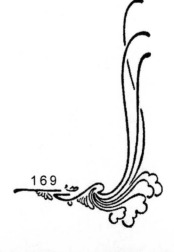

"For every minute
you remain angry,
you give up sixty seconds
of peace of mind."

~ Ralph Waldo Emerson

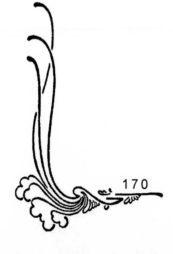

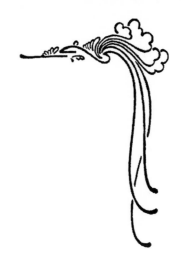

"For hope is but the dream
of those that wake."

~ Matthew Prior

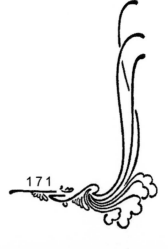

"Forgiveness
does not change the past,
but it does enlarge
the future."

~ Les Brown

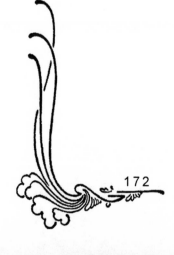

"*Freedom isn't worth having
if it doesn't include
the freedom
to make mistakes.*"

~ Mahatma Gandhi

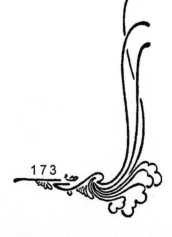

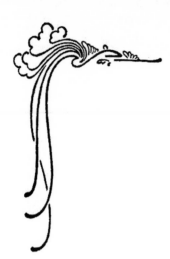

"*Friends are the sailors
who guide your rickety boat
safely across
the dangerous waters of life.*"

~ Unknown

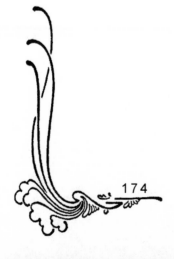

"Give to the world
the best you have
and the best
will come back to you."

~ Madeline Bridges

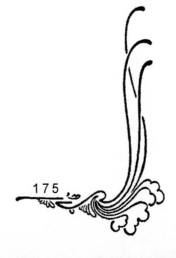

"Go as far as you can see;
when you get there
you'll be able to see farther."

~ Thomas Carlyle

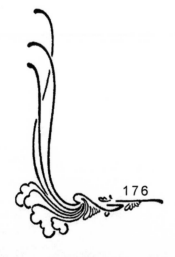

"God gave you a gift
of 86,400 seconds today.
Have you used one to say
'thank you'?"

~ William Arthur Ward

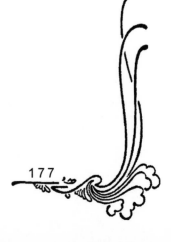

*"Good business leaders
create a vision,
articulate the vision,
passionately own the vision,
and relentlessly drive it
to completion."*

~ Jack Welch

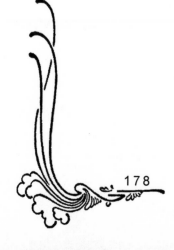

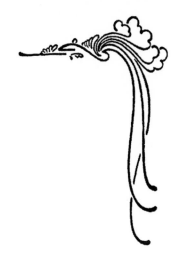

"*Good humor*
*is one of the preservatives*
*of our peace*
*and tranquility.*"

~ Thomas Jefferson

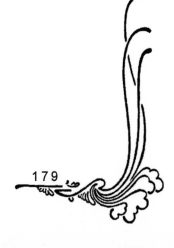

"*Good manners
will open doors
that the best education
cannot.*"

~ Clarence Thomas

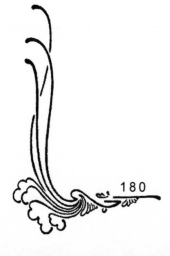

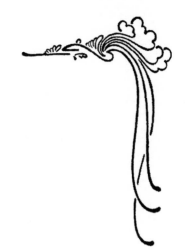

"Grace comes out of nowhere.
It can happen at any time,
at any place."

~ Mātā Amṛtānandamayī Devī "Amma"

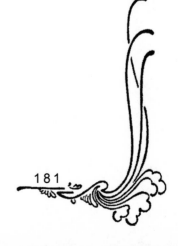

"*Great minds discuss ideas.*
*Average minds*
*discuss events.*
*Small minds*
*discuss people.*"

~ Eleanor Roosevelt

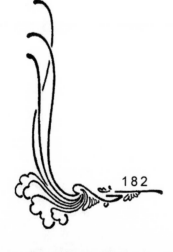

*"Great Spirit brings together
and maintains together
those who belong together
in love."*

~ Buffalo Roaming via Dea Shandera

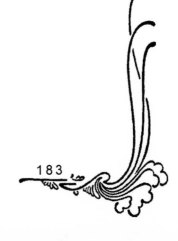

*"Happiness arises
in a state of peace,
not of tumult."*

~ Ann Radcliffe

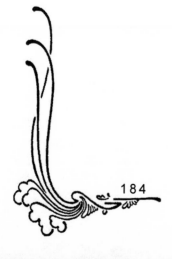

"Happiness is not achieved
by the conscious pursuit
of happiness;
it is generally the by-product
of other activities."

~ Aldous Huxley

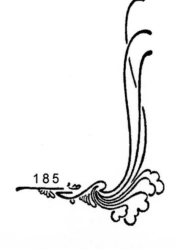

"*Happiness is not something ready made. It comes from your own actions.*"

~ HH The Dalai Lama

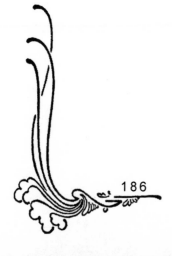

"*Happiness will never come
to those who fail
to appreciate
what they already have.*"

~ Unknown

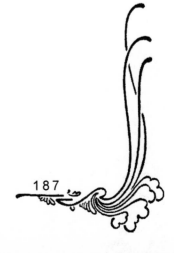

"*Hatred is like wet cement.*
*The longer you stay in it,*
*the harder it will be*

*for you to get out of it.*
*So Stay HAPPY!!!*"

~ Unknown

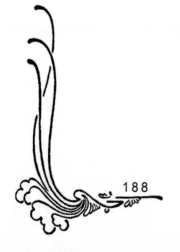

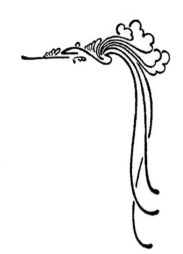

"Have you ever noticed?
Anybody going slower than
you is an idiot,
And anyone going faster
than you is a maniac."

~ George Carlin

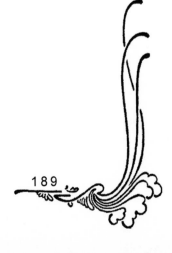

*"Having a goal
is a state of happiness."*

~ F. J. Barrek

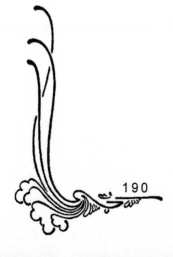

"He who asks
is a fool for five minutes,
but he who does not ask
remains a fool forever."

~ Chinese Proverb

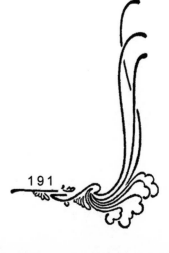

"*He who lives
in harmony with himself
lives in harmony
with the universe.*"

~ Marcus Aurelius

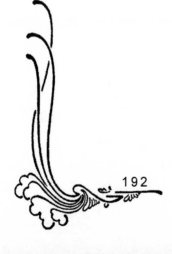

"He who refuses
to learn from history
is forced
to repeat its mistakes."

~ Ravi Zacharias

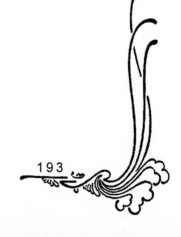

"Here is a test to find
whether your mission
on Earth is finished:
If you're alive, it isn't."

~ Richard Bach

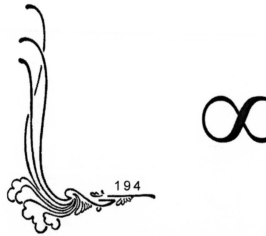

"History teaches us
that men and nations
behave wisely
once they have exhausted
all other alternatives."

~ Abba Eban

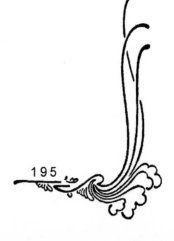

*"Hold up your head!*
*You were not made*
*for failure.*
*You were made for victory.*
*Go forward*
*with a joyful confidence."*

~ George Elliot

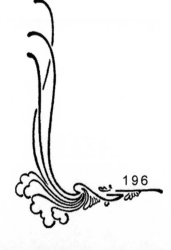

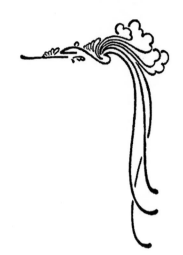

"Holding onto anger
is like grasping onto
a hot coal with the intent
of throwing it at someone else.
You are the one
who gets burned."

~ Buddha

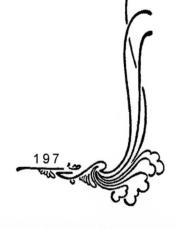

"Hope
is a waking dream."

~ Aristotle

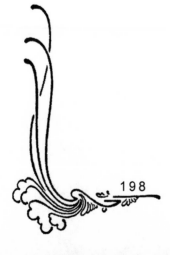

"Hope is like a bird
that senses the dawn
and starts to sing
while it is still dark."

~ Unknown

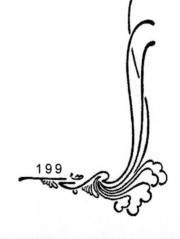

"Hope is like a road
in the country;
there was never a road
but when many people
walk on it,
the road comes into existence."

~ Lin Yutang

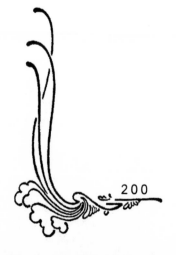

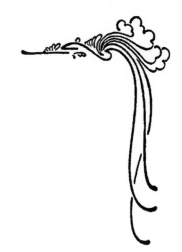

"Hope is the dream
of a person awake."

~ French Proverb

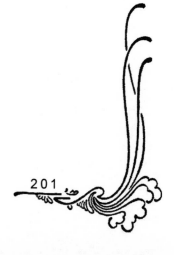

"Hope is the thing
with feathers that perches
in the soul and sings
the tune without words
and never stops."

~ Emily Dickinson

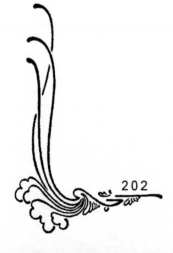

"How does one become
a butterfly?
You must want to fly
so much that you are
willing to give up being
a caterpillar."

~ Trina Paulus

"How people treat you
is their karma;
how you react is yours."

~ Wayne Dyer

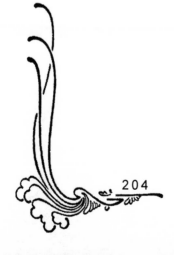

"I consider myself
a Hindu, Christian,
Muslim, Jew, Buddhist
and Confucian."

~ Mahatma Gandhi

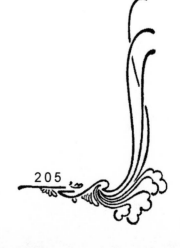

*"I do not count*
*the hours I spend*
*in wandering by the sea."*

~ Ralph Waldo Emerson

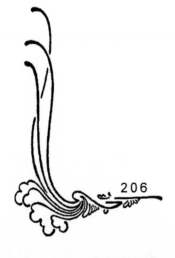

"*I do not give lectures
or a little charity.
When I give,
I give myself.*"

~ Walt Whitman

"I don't know
the key to success,
but the key to failure
is trying to please everybody."

~ Bill Cosby

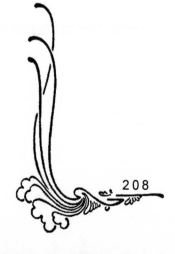

*"I found the best light
in the dark."*

~ Arturo Macias Uceda

"I had the blues
because I had no shoes
until upon the street,
I met a man
who had no feet."

~ Denis Waitely

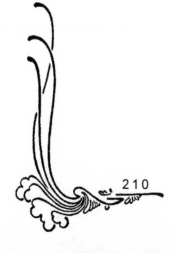

"I have found
the best way to give advice
to your children is
to find out what they want
and then advise them
to do it."

~ Harry Truman

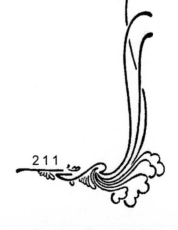

*"I have had dreams
and I have had nightmares,
but I have conquered
my nightmares
because of my dreams."*

~ Jonas Salk

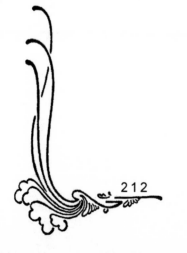

"*I have just three things*
*to teach:*
*simplicity, patience, compassion.*
*These three are*
*your greatest treasures.*"

~ Lao Tzu

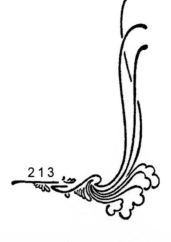

"I have learnt silence
from the talkative,
toleration from the intolerant,
and kindness
from the unkind."

~ Kahlil Gibran

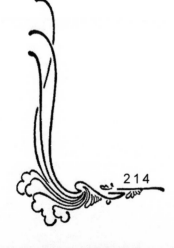

"I have no fear that
the result of our experiment
will be that men
may be trusted
to govern themselves
without a master."

~ Thomas Jefferson

*"The price of greatness
is responsibility."*

~ Sir Winston Churchill

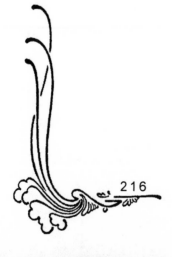

"I have not failed.
I've just found
10,000 ways
that won't work."

~ Thomas Edison

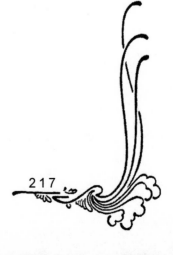

"I know
of no more encouraging fact
than the unquestionable
ability of man
to elevate his life
by conscious endeavor."

~ Henry David Thoreau

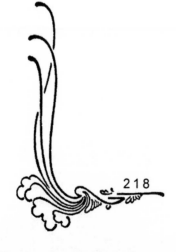

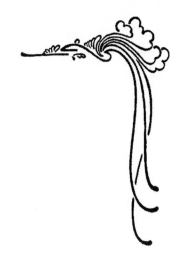

"I understand democracy
as something that gives
the weak the same chance
as the strong."

~ Mahatma Gandhi

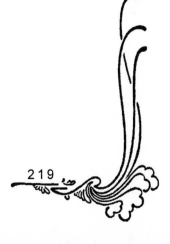

*"I wonder how many people I've looked at all my life and never seen."*

~ John Steinbeck

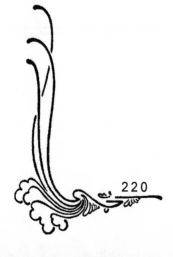

"Your task
is not to seek for love,
but merely to seek and find
all the barriers within yourself
that you have built against it."

~ Jalāl ad-Dīn Muhammad Balkhī "Rumi"

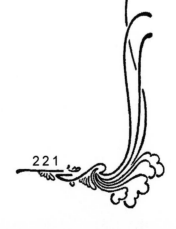

"If everyone
is moving forward together,
then success takes care of itself."

~ Henry Ford

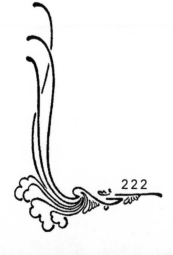

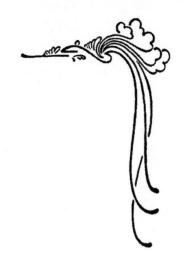

"If I had a single flower
for every time
I think about you,
I could walk forever
in my garden."

~ Unknown

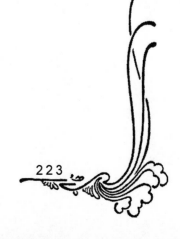

*"If life is so blue
then select another color
from the rainbow."*

~ Unknown

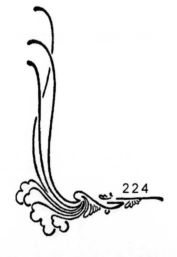

"If opportunity
doesn't knock, build a door."

~ Milton Berle

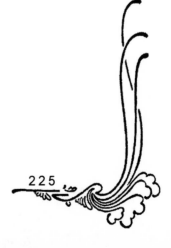

"Children are the world's
most valuable resource
and its best hope
for the future."

~ John F. Kennedy

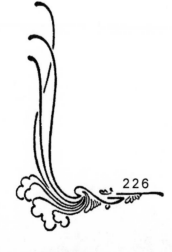

"If the success
or failure of this planet
and of human beings
depended on how I am
and what I do,
how would I be?
What would I do?"

~ Buckminster Fuller

*"If there is anything
that a man can do well,
I say let him do it.
Give him a chance."*

~ Abraham Lincoln

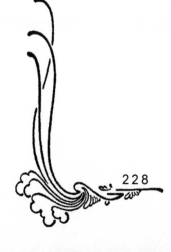

"*If there must be trouble
let it be in my day,
that my child
may have peace.*"

~ Thomas Paine

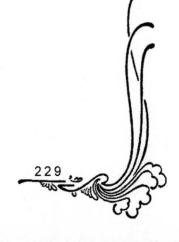

"If they can make penicillin
out of moldy bread,
they can sure make something
out of you."

~ Muhammad Ali

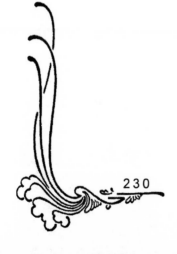

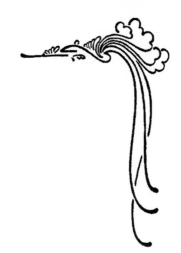

*"If you can do one thing
you thought was impossible,
it causes you to rethink
your beliefs."*

~ Anthony Robbins

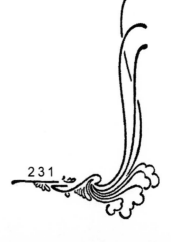

"If you don't like something,
change it.
If you can't change it,
change your attitude."

~ Maya Angelou

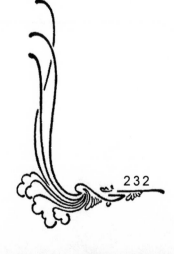

"*If we could see the miracle
of a single flower clearly,
our whole life would change.*"

~ Anonymous

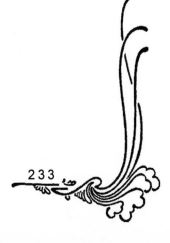

"If you are excited
and blissful,
you send a positive vibe.
If you are cranky
and irritated,
you send negative vibes.
Only you can control it."

~ Unknown

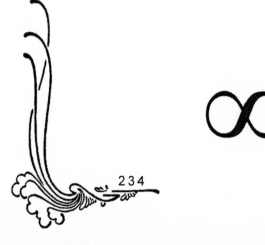

234

"Think of a person
you're angry at
and consciously decide
to let it go.
Free your mind
so more joy can flow in."

~ Brent N. Hunter

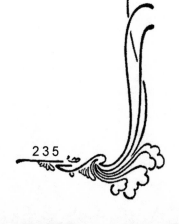

*"If you are not fulfilled,
it may be because
you are not pursuing
your destiny."*

~ Anthony Chisom

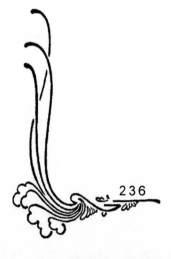

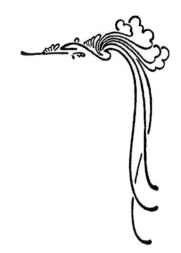

"If you can give your son
or daughter only one gift,
let it be enthusiasm."

~ Bruce Barton

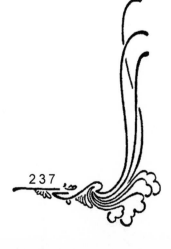

"*If you can imagine it,
you can create it.
If you can dream it,
you can become it.*"

~ William Arthur Ward

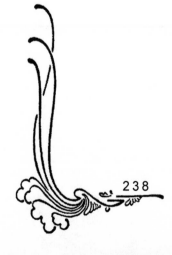

238

"*If you correct your mind,
the rest of your life
will fall into place.*"

~ Lao Tzu

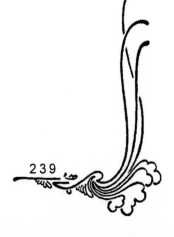

*"If you do not hope,
you will not find
what is beyond your hopes."*

~ St. Clement of Alexandria

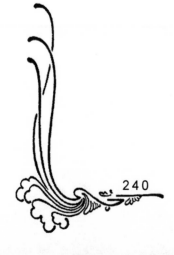

"We must pursue
peaceful ends
through peaceful means."

~ Martin Luther King, Jr.

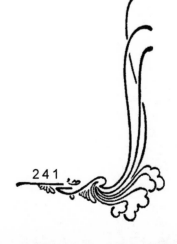

"If you follow your bliss,
doors will open for you
that wouldn't have opened
for anyone else."

~ Joseph Campbell

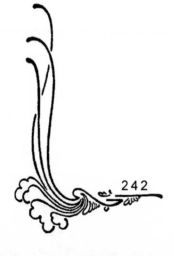

242

"If you have a dog,
get a cat.
If you have a cat,
get a dog.
Switch things around,
see miracles
where you haven't before."

~ Brent N. Hunter

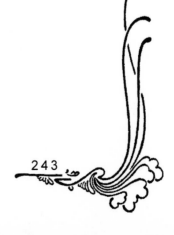

"What you seek
is seeking you."

~ Jalāl ad-Dīn Muhammad Balkhī "Rumi"

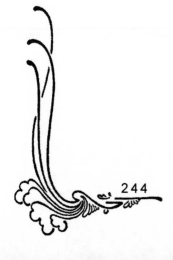

"If you judge people,
you have no time
to love them."

~ Mother Teresa

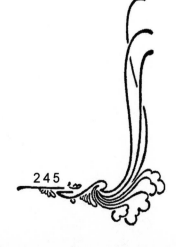

*"If you realized
how powerful
your thoughts are,
you would never think
a negative thought again."*

~ Peace Pilgrim

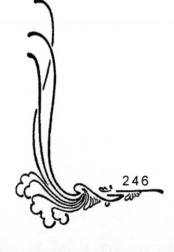

"If you turn it over
to the universe,
you will be surprised
and dazzled by
what is delivered."

~ Unknown

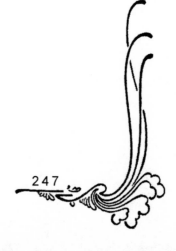

"If you want more joy, serve.
If you want more money,
solve problems.
If you want more freedom,
face your fears."

~ Unknown

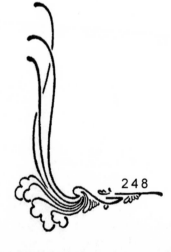

"*If you want others
to be happy,
practice compassion.
If you want to be happy,
practice compassion.*"

~ HH The Dalai Lama

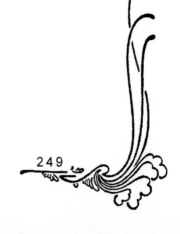

"*If you want to make peace,
you don't talk to
your friends.
You talk to your enemies.*"

~ Moshe Dayan

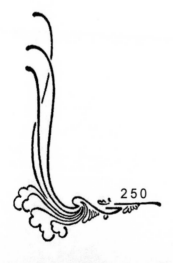

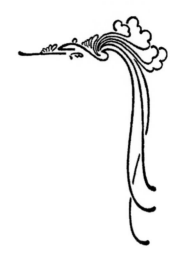

"*If you would know
strength and patience,
welcome the company
of trees.*"

~ Hal Borland

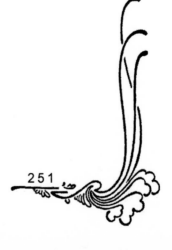

"If you're bored with life,
or you don't get up
every morning with a burning
desire to do things,
you don't have
enough goals."

~ Lou Holtz

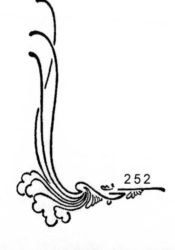

"If you're not making
someone else's life better,
then you're wasting
your time."

~ Will Smith

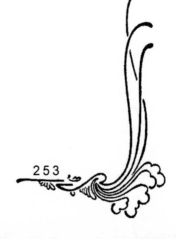

"I'm a great believer
in luck and I find
the harder I work
the more I have of it."

~ Thomas Jefferson

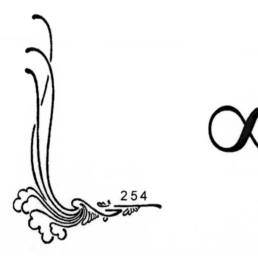

"*Imagination is more important than knowledge.*"

~ Albert Einstein

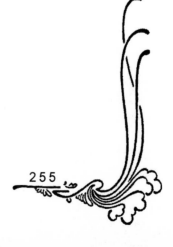

"*Imagination
is the beginning of creation.
You imagine what you desire,
you will what you imagine
and at last you create
what you will.*"

~ George Bernard Shaw

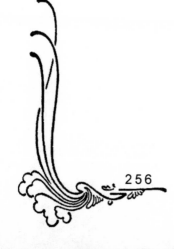

"*Imagination
is the one weapon
in the war against reality.*"

~ Jules de Gaultier

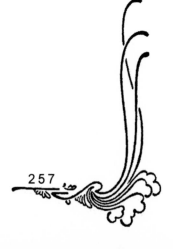

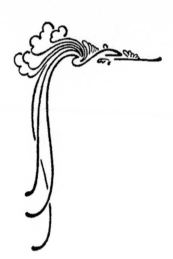

*"Impossible*
*is an opinion."*

~ Brent C.J. Britton

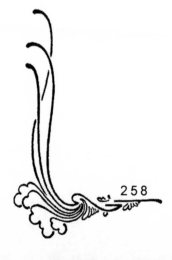

"*Impossible is not a declaration. It's a dare.*"

~ Muhammad Ali

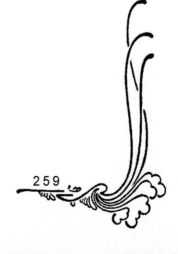

*"Improvement begins with 'I.'"*

~ Arnold H. Glasow

∞

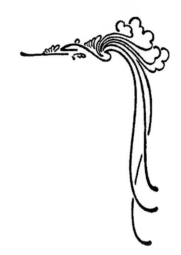

"In a democracy,
dissent is an act of faith."

~ J. William Fulbright

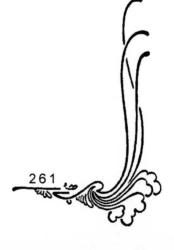

"In a democracy,
the individual enjoys
not only the ultimate power
but carries
the ultimate responsibility."

~ Norman Cousins

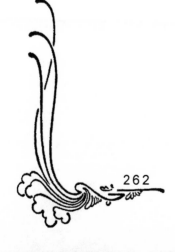

"In a time
of universal deceit,
telling the truth
is a revolutionary act."

~ George Orwell

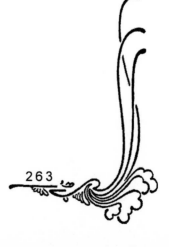

"In a world
of infinite possibilities,
it is irresponsible
to be pessimistic."

~ Brent N. Hunter

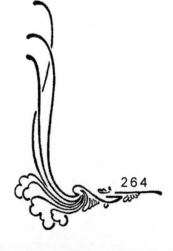

*"Don't let what you cannot do interfere with what you can do."*

~ John Wooden

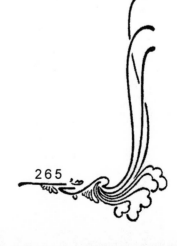

265

*"In case of doubt,
it is best to lean to the side
of mercy."*

~ Legal Proverb

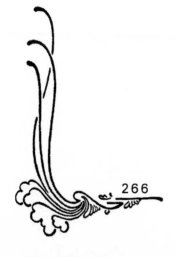

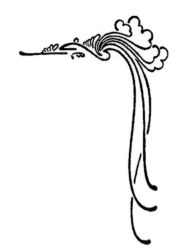

"In making new choices,
be aware of how people
are positively, negatively,
or neutrally affecting you."

~ Unknown

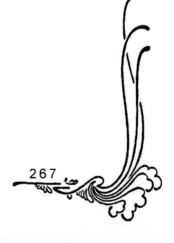

"The biggest adventure
you can take
is to live the life
of your dreams."

~ Oprah Winfrey

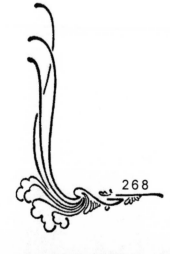

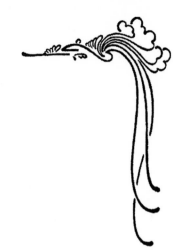

"In oneself
lies the whole world,
and if you know how
to look and learn,
the door is there and the key
is in your hand."

~ Krishnamurti

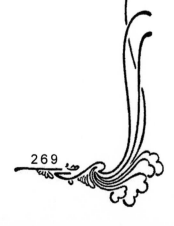

"*In order to succeed,
your desire for success
should be greater
than your fear of failure.*"

~ Bill Cosby

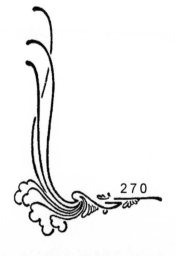

"In the case of good books,
the point is not to see
how many of them
you can get through,
but how many
can get through to you."

~ Mortimer J. Adler

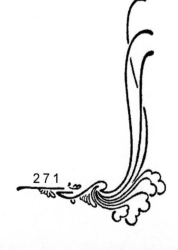

"In the cookies of life,
your friends are
the chocolate chips."

~ Unknown

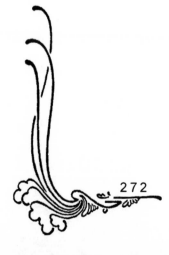

"In the evening of life,
we will be judged
on love alone."

~ St. John of the Cross

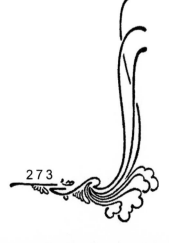

"In the hopes
of reaching the moon,
men fail to see
the flowers that blossom
at their feet."

~ Albert Schweitzer

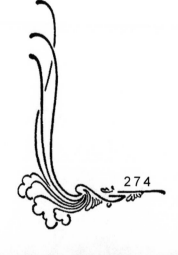

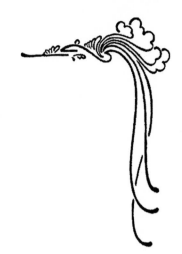

"In the middle of difficulty
lies opportunity."

~ Albert Einstein

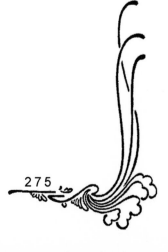

*"In this world
man must either be anvil
or hammer."*

~ Henry Wadsworth Longfellow

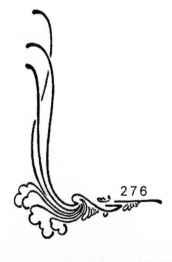

"In true love
the smallest distance
is too great,
and the greatest distance
can be bridged."

~ Hans Nouwens

"Inaction breeds doubt and fear.
Action breeds confidence
and courage."

~ Dale Carnegie

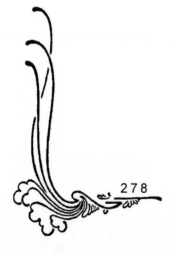

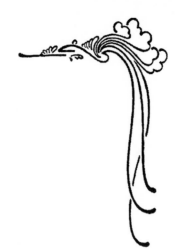

*"Individually, we are one drop. Together, we are an ocean."*

~ Ryunosuke Satoro

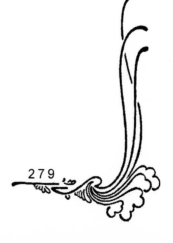

*"Individuals play the game, but teams beat the odds."*

~ SEAL Team saying

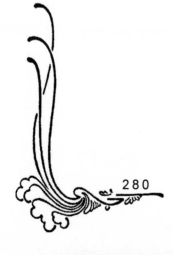

"*Instinct is the nose of the mind.*"

~ Madame De Girardin

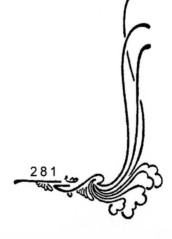

281

*"It always seems impossible until it's done."*

~ Nelson Mandela

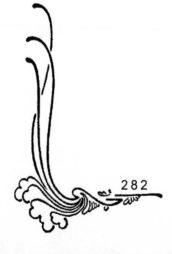

"It does not matter
how slowly you go
so long as you do not stop."

~ Confucius

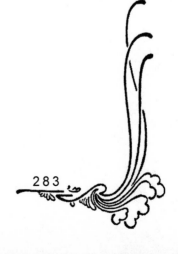

"It doesn't matter
where you are coming from.
All that matters
is where you are going."

~ Brian Tracy

"It doesn't matter
who you are
or where you come from.
The ability to triumph
begins with you.
Always."

~ Unknown

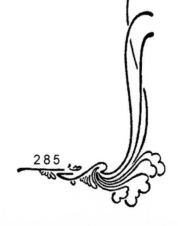

"*It is absurd
to divide people
into good and bad.
People are either charming
or tedious.*"

~ Oscar Wilde

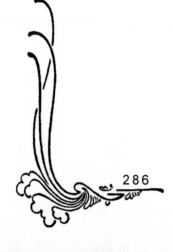

286

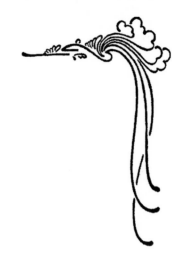

*"It is difficult,*
*but not impossible,*
*to conduct*
*strictly honest business."*

~ Mahatma Gandhi

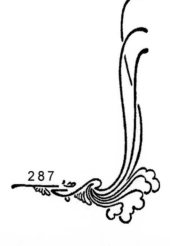

*"It is in your moments*
*of decision*
*that your destiny is shaped."*

~ Anthony Robbins

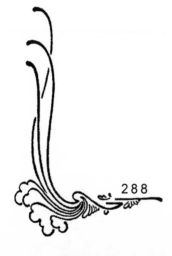

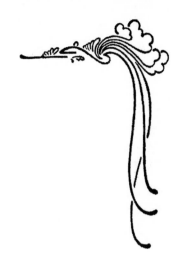

"*It is never too late to be who you might have been.*"

~ George Elliot

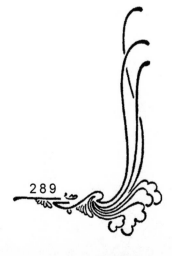

"It is never too late
to give up our prejudices."

~ Henry David Thoreau

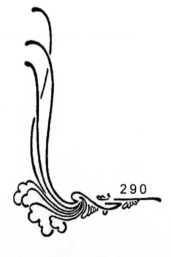

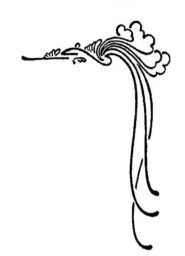

"It is not enough
to stare up the steps,
we must step up the stairs."

~ Václav Havel

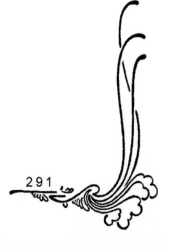

"*It is not only
for what we do
that we are held responsible,
but also
for what we don't do.*"

~ Moliere

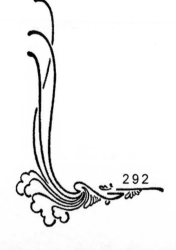

"It is not up to
President Obama
to solve our problems,
WE must solve them.
When the people lead,
the leaders follow."

~ Brent N. Hunter

293

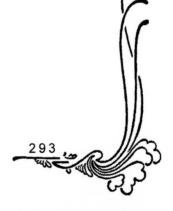

"It is not who is right,
but what is right,
that is of importance."

~ Thomas Huxley

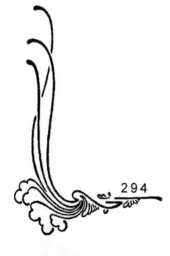

294

"It is the friends
you can call up at 4AM
that matter."

~ Marlene Dietrich

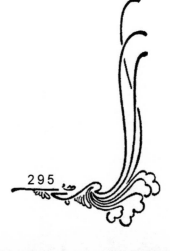

"It is the mark
of an educated mind
to be able to entertain
a thought
without accepting it."

~ Aristotle

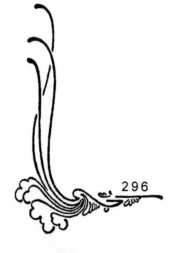

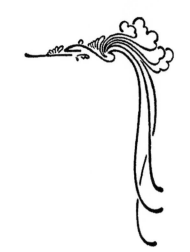

"It isn't enough
to talk about peace,
one must believe it.
And it isn't enough
to believe in it,
one must work for it."

~ Eleanor Roosevelt

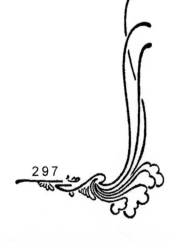

*"It only takes a moment for a miracle to happen."*

~ Unknown

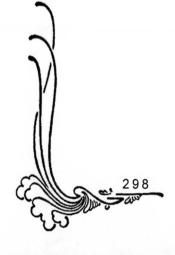

"I was, and I am.
So shall I be
to the end of time,
for I am without end."

~ Kahlil Gibran

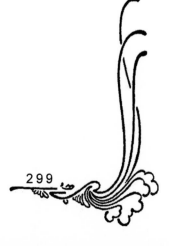

"It takes a long time
to grow an old friend."

~ John Leonard

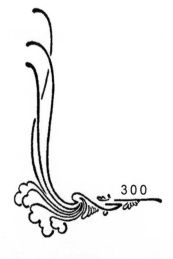

"It's better
to stir up a question
without deciding it
than to decide it
without stirring it up."

~ Joseph Joubert

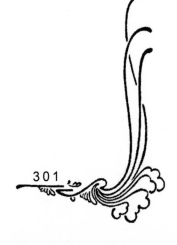

"It's easy to make a buck.
It's a lot tougher
to make a difference."

~ Tom Brokaw

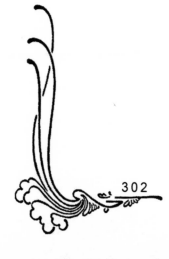

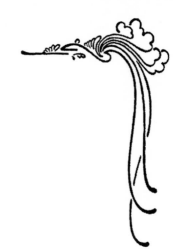

"It's not true
that nice guys finish last.
Nice guys are winners
before the game even starts."

~ Addison Walker

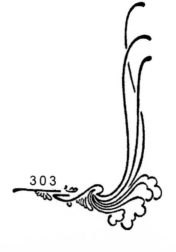

*"It's not what you look at
that matters,
it's what you see."*

~ Henry David Thoreau

"*It's time to start living the life we've imagined.*"

~ Henry James

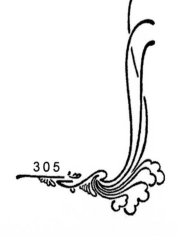

"I've found that luck
is quite predictable.
If you want more luck,
take more chances.
Be more active.
Show up more often."

~ Brian Tracy

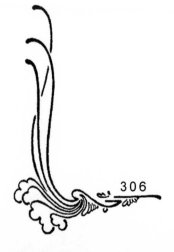

*"Just as a teacher cannot give their knowledge away by teaching, you cannot give away all your love by loving."*

~ Brent N. Hunter

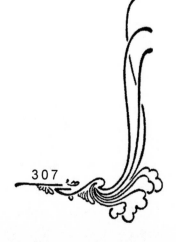

*"Just because a man lacks the use of his eyes doesn't mean he lacks vision."*

~ Stevie Wonder

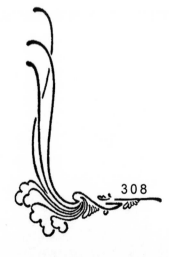

"God wants spiritual fruits,
not religious nuts."

~ From an old T-shirt of mine

"*Just remember,
when you think all is lost,
the future remains.*"

~ Robert H. Goddard

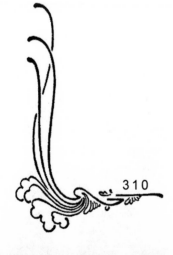

"Just when we think
the door has closed,
light floods through
the window."

~ Unknown

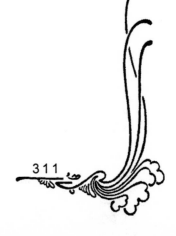

"*Keep your face
to the sunshine,
and you cannot see the shadow.*"

~ Helen Keller

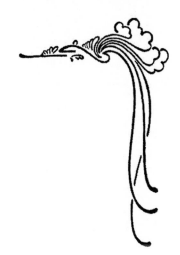

"*Keep your fears to yourself,
but share your courage
with others.*"

~ Robert Louis Stevenson

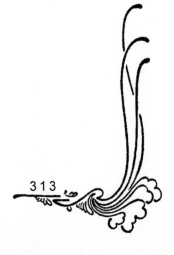

"Kind words
can be short and easy
to speak, but their echoes
are truly endless."

~ Mother Teresa

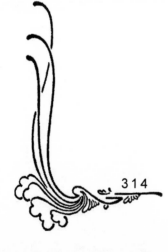

*"Kind words*
*will unlock an iron door."*

~ Turkish Proverb

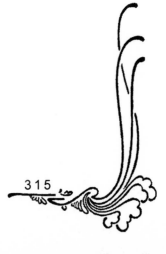

"*Kindness is the language
which the deaf can hear
and the blind can see.*"

~ Mark Twain

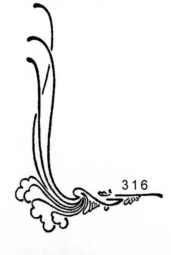

316

*"Knowledge talks, wisdom listens."*

~ Unknown

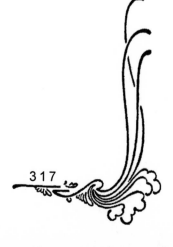

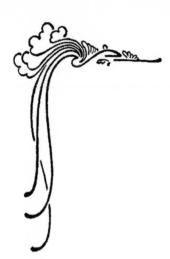

"*Laughter is the sun that drives winter from the human face.*"

~ Victor Hugo

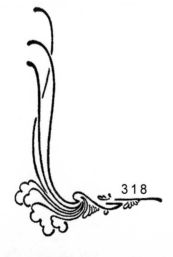

"*Lead into the light,*
*not out of the darkness.*"

~ Unknown

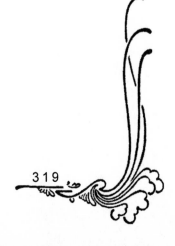

"Learn from yesterday,
live for today,
hope for tomorrow.
The important thing
is to not stop questioning."

~ Albert Einstein

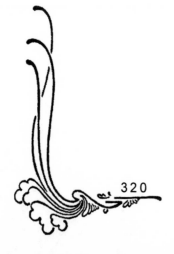

"Learn to calm down
the winds of your mind,
and you will enjoy
great inner peace."

~ Remez Sasson

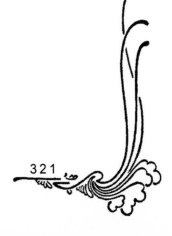

*"Learn to listen,*
*for then you shall be heard."*

~ Unknown

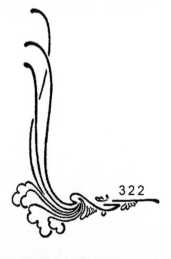

322

"Learning is finding out
what you already know.
Doing is demonstrating
that you know it."

~ Richard Bach

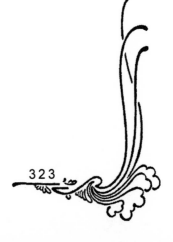

*"Let no one ever come to you
without leaving better
and happier."*

~ Mother Teresa

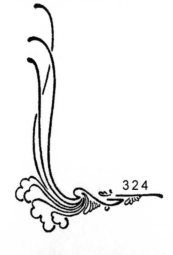

"*Let the beauty of the wild
leave footprints
on your heart.*"

~ Peggy Anderson

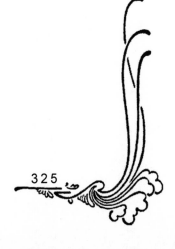

"*Let us be grateful to people who make us happy: they are the charming gardeners who make our souls blossom.*"

~ Marcel Proust

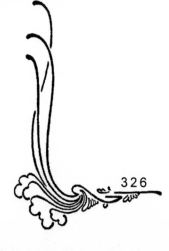

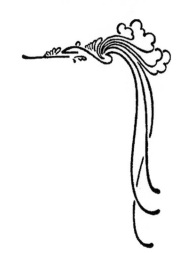

"*Let us never negotiate*
*out of fear.*
*But let us never fear*
*to negotiate.*"

~ John F. Kennedy

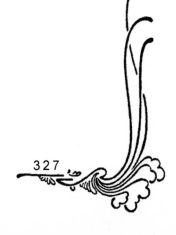

"Tonight,
when you are drifting
off to sleep,
instead of counting sheep,
count blessings."

~ Brent N. Hunter

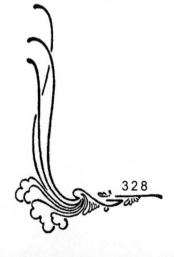

"Breathe. Let go.
And remind yourself
that this moment
is the only one you know
you have for sure."

~ Oprah Winfrey

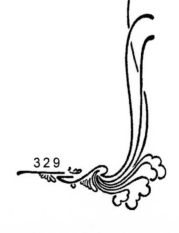

"*Let us not wallow
in the valley of despair.*"

~ Martin Luther King, Jr.

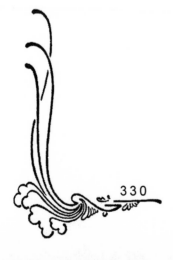

"*Let us put our minds together and see what life we can make for our children.*"

~ Sitting Bull

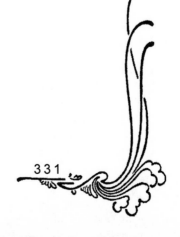

"*Let us train our minds
to desire what the situation
demands.*"

~ Seneca

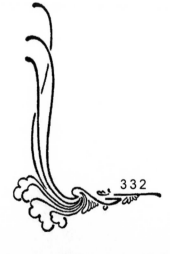

332

"*Let your hopes, not your hurts,
shape your future.*"

~ Robert H. Schuller

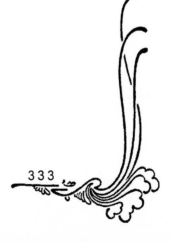

*"Life is a grindstone.
Whether it grinds us down
or polishes us up
depends on us."*

~ Thomas L. Holdcroft

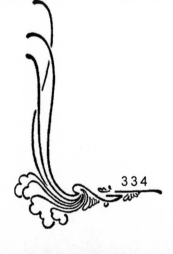

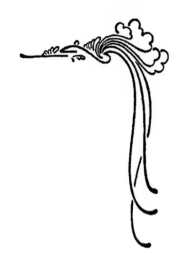

"*Life is a promise;
fulfill it.*"

~ Mother Teresa

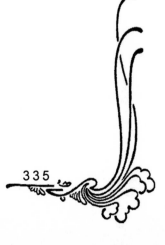

*"Life is an echo;
what you send out comes back."*

~ Chinese proverb

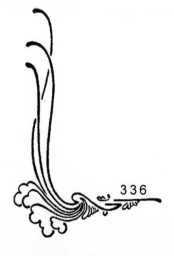

*"Life is like riding a bicycle. To keep your balance, you must keep moving."*

~ Albert Einstein

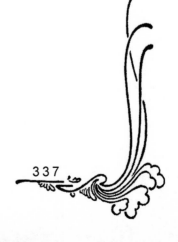

"Life is not about waiting
for the storms to pass...
it's about learning to dance
in the rain!"

~ Vivian Greene

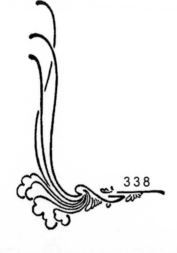

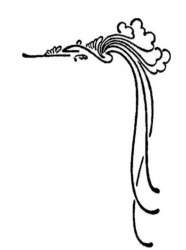

"*Life is not so short*
*but that there is*
*always time enough*
*for courtesy.*"

~ Ralph Waldo Emerson

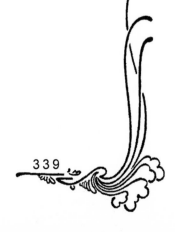

"Life is short,
break the rules, caress slowly,
forgive quickly, smile and say
hello to the stranger
on the street."

~ Unknown

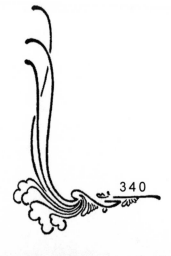

"Life is too short,
so kiss slowly,
laugh insanely, love truly
and forgive quickly."

~ Unknown

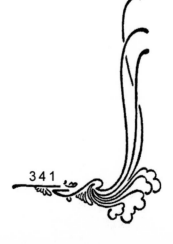

*"Fear invites you to play, for it can't play alone. Alone, it has nowhere to go and nothing to do."*

~ Bill Froehlich,
Filmmaker and Co-author of U R The Solution

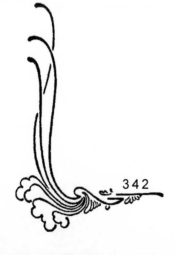

342

"*Life was really so much easier when Apple and BlackBerry were just fruits!*"

~ Unknown

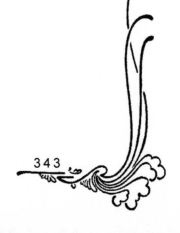

"*Life without liberty
is like a body without spirit.*"

~ Kahlil Gibran

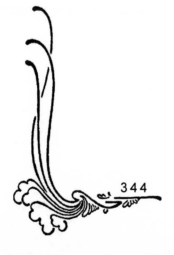

*"Life would be so much easier if we only had the source code."*

~ Unknown

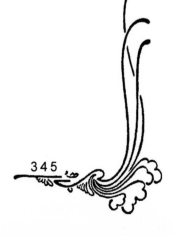

"Life's challenges
are not supposed to
paralyze you,
they're supposed to help you
discover who you are."

~ Ronald Reagan

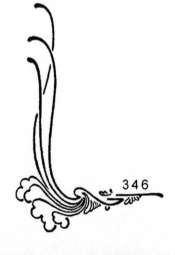

"*Life's most persistent
and urgent question is
what are you doing for others?*"

~ Martin Luther King, Jr.

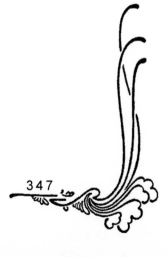

*"Listen to the sound
of your soul.
The truth of your destiny
lives in your heart."*

~ Adele Basheer

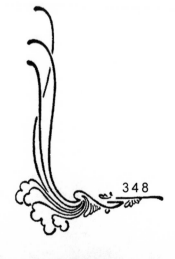

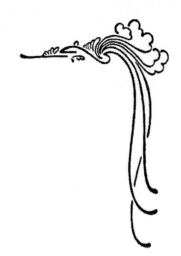

"*Live out of your imagination,
not your history.*"

~ Stephen Covey

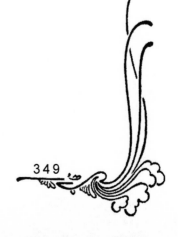

"Look at life through
the windshield,
not the rearview mirror."

~ Byrd Baggett

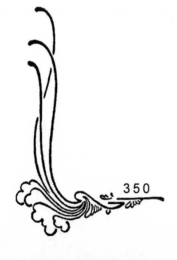

350

"*Look behind
every once in a while,
but spend most of our time
looking forward
and avoiding
potential disasters ahead.*"

~ Brent N. Hunter

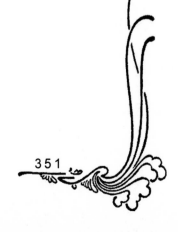

351

*"Lose your head
and come to your senses."*

~ Fritz Perls

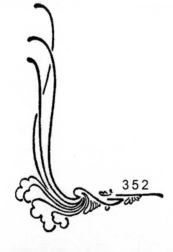

352

"*Love and compassion
are necessities, not luxuries.
Without them
humanity cannot survive.*"

~ HH The Dalai Lama

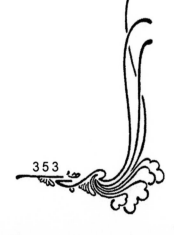

"*Love and kindness
are never wasted.
They always make a difference.
They bless the one
who receives
and they bless you, the giver.*"

~ Barbara De Angelis

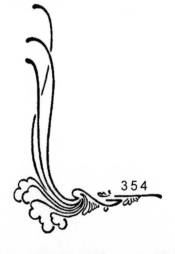

354

"*Love as if world peace*
*depended upon it*
*— it just might!*"

~ Brent N. Hunter

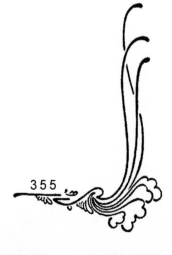

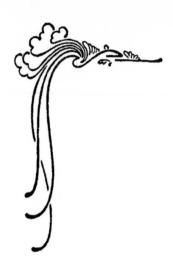

"Do not be satisfied
with the stories
that come before you.
Unfold your own myth."

~ Jalāl ad-Dīn Muhammad Balkhī "Rumi"

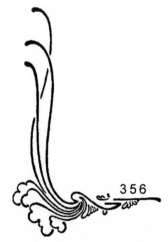

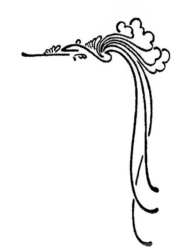

*"Love builds bridges where there are none."*

~ Unknown

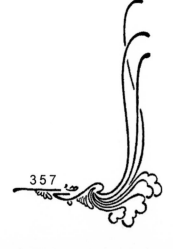

"*Love is like a butterfly —
it goes where it pleases
and it pleases wherever it goes.*"

~ Unknown

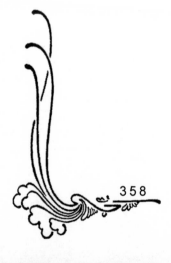

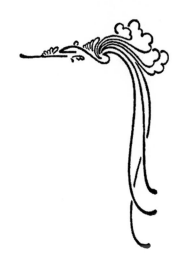

*"Love is our true essence.*
*We are all beads*
*on the same thread of love."*

~ Mātā Amṛtānandamayī Devī "Amma"

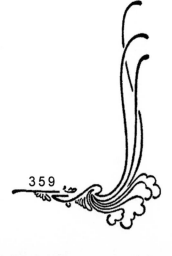

*"Love isn't always a feeling,
it is often a deliberate act.
Make a difference
by performing acts of love."*

~ Brent N. Hunter

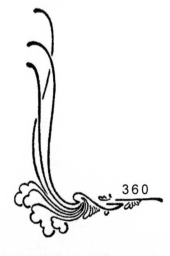

"*Love makes your soul
crawl out from its hiding place.*"

~ Zora Neale Hurston

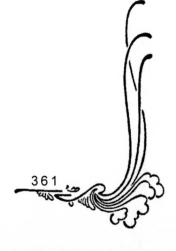

"*Love yourself and others
as if world peace
depended upon it,
because it does!*"

~ Brent N. Hunter

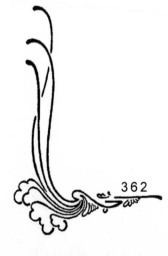

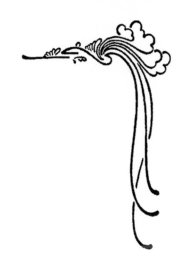

"*Make the most of yourself,
for that is all there is of you.*"

~ Ralph Waldo Emerson

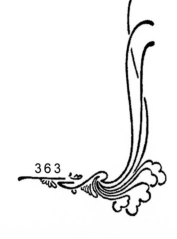

*"Mankind must put an end
to war or war will put an end
to mankind."*

~ John F. Kennedy

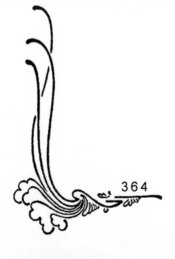

364

"Many of life's failures
are people who didn't realize
how close they were to success
when they gave up."

~ Thomas Edison

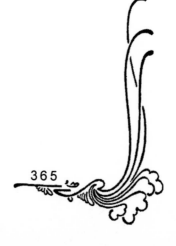

"*Begin to see yourself
as a soul with a body
rather than a body with a soul.*"

~ Wayne Dyer

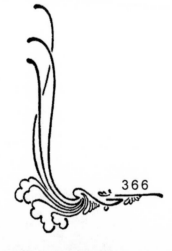

366

"May our heart's garden
of awakening bloom with
hundreds of flowers."

~ Thich Nhât Hanh

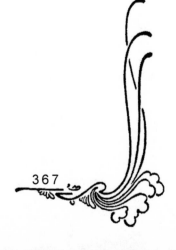

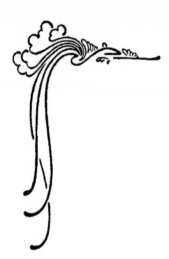

"*Meet success like a gentleman and disaster like a man.*"

~ Frederick Edwin Smith, Lord Birkenhead

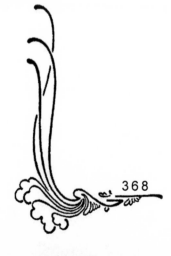

"Men are at war
with each other because
each man is at war
with himself."

~ Francis Meehan

369

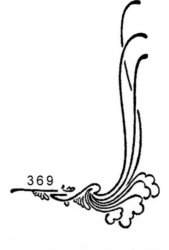

"Minds are like parachutes
— they function best
when they are open."

~ Unknown

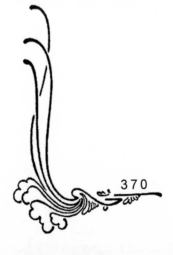

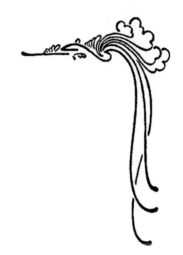

"*Live quietly in the moment
and see the beauty before you —
the future
will take care of itself.*"

~ Paramahansa Yogananda

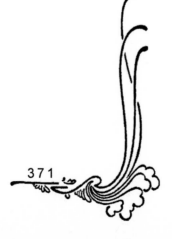

"*Mistakes, obviously,
show us what needs improving.
Without mistakes,
how would we know
what we had to work on?*"

~ Peter McWilliams

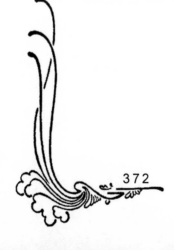

"Money is like manure:
it's not worth a thing
unless it's spread around
encouraging young things
to grow."

~ Thornton Wilder

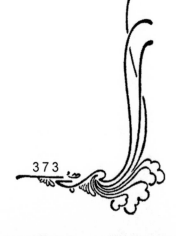

"Most folks
are about as happy
as they make up their minds
to be."

~ Abraham Lincoln

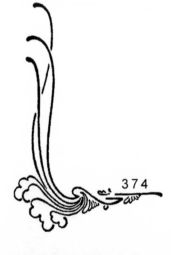

374

"Most of our obstacles
would melt away if,
instead of cowering before them,
we should make up our
minds to walk boldly
through them."

~ Orison Swett Marden

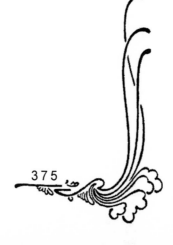

"*Most of us
have far more courage
than we ever dreamed possible.*"

~ Dale Carnegie

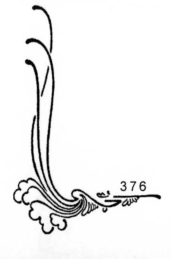

376

"*Most people don't plan to fail,*
*they fail to plan.*"

~ Unknown

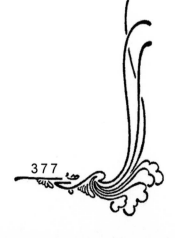

"*Motivation
is what gets you started.
Habit is what keeps you going.*"

~ Jim Rohn

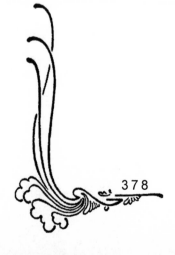

*"Use your mind
to go beyond your mind."*

~ Brent N. Hunter

379

"*Music fills the infinite between two souls.*"

~ Rabindranath Tagore

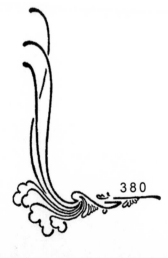

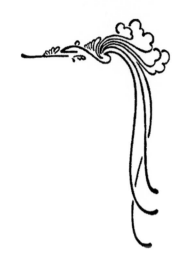

"My life is my message."

~ Mahatma Gandhi

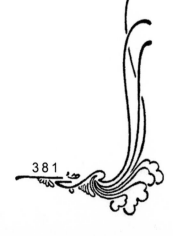

"We are still masters
of our fate.
We are still captains
of our souls."

~ Sir Winston Churchill

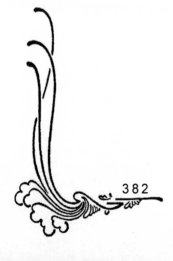

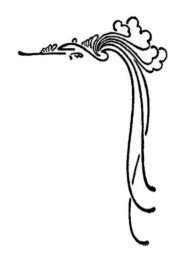

"*My religion is kindness.*"

~ HH The Dalai Lama

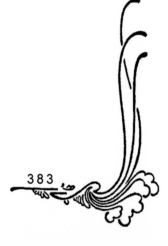

"*My religion is love and service.*"

~ Mātā Amṛtānandamayī Devī "Amma"

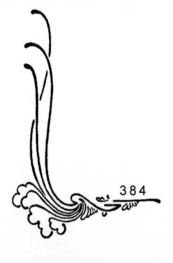

"My soul
can find no staircase
to heaven unless it be through
Earth's loveliness."

~ Michelangelo

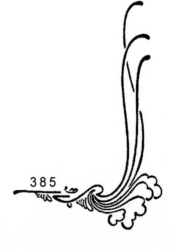

"*Never confuse a single defeat
with a final defeat.*"

~ F. Scott Fitzgerald

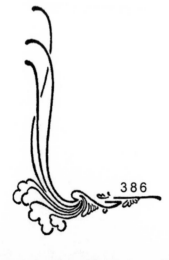

386

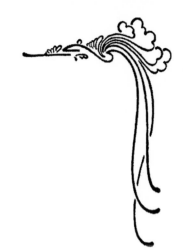

*"Never give up on something
that you can't go a day
without thinking about."*

~ Unknown

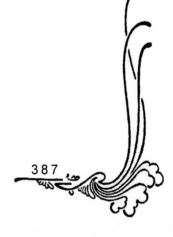

"Never look down
on anybody unless
you're helping him up."

~ Jesse Jackson

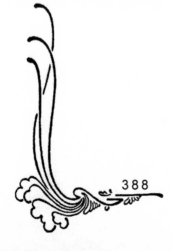

388

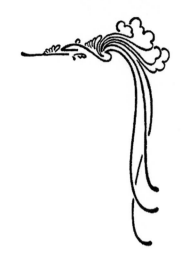

"Never lose an opportunity
of seeing anything
that is beautiful.
Welcome it in every face,
in every sky, in every shower."

~ Ralph Waldo Emerson

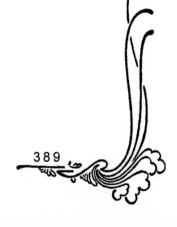

389

"No one can go back and make
a brand new start,
but anyone can start now
and make a brand new ending."

~ Nigel Risner

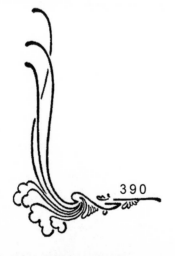

"Thousands of candles
can be lighted
from a single candle,
and the life of the candle
will not be shortened.
Happiness never decreases
by being shared."

~ Buddha

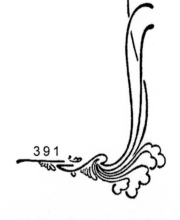

"*No one cares
how much you know,
until they know how much
you care.*"

~ Don Swartz

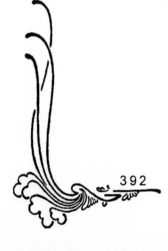

"No one is useless in this world
who lightens the burdens
of another."

~ Charles Dickens

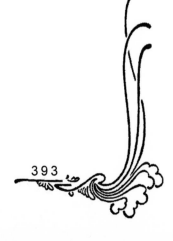

"No person ever injured
his or her eyesight
looking on the bright side
of things."

~ Unknown

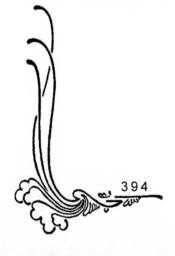

394

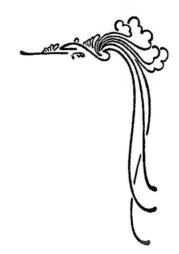

"No road is long
with good company."

~ Turkish Proverb

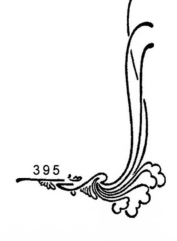

"No, we are not satisfied,
and we will not be satisfied
until justice rolls down
like water and righteousness
like a mighty stream."

~ Martin Luther King, Jr.

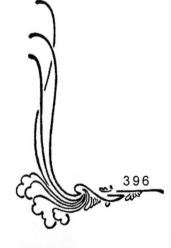

"*Nobody
can make you feel inferior
without your consent.*"

~ Eleanor Roosevelt

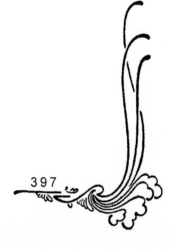

"Nobody knows the age
of the human race,
but everybody agrees
that it is old enough
to know better."

~ Anonymous

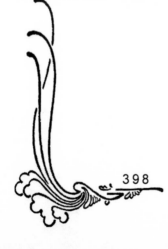

"Nodding the head
does not row the boat."

~ Irish Proverb

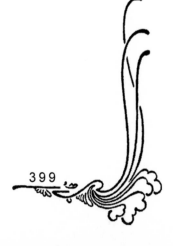

"Non-cooperation
is a measure of discipline
and sacrifice,
and it demands respect
for the opposite views."

~ Mahatma Gandhi

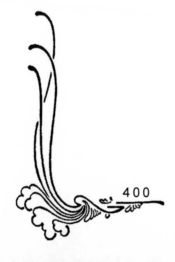

400

"None of us
is as smart as all of us."

~ Ken Blanchard

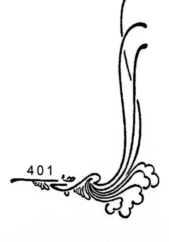

*"Not everything that counts can be counted, and not everything that can be counted counts."*

~ Albert Einstein

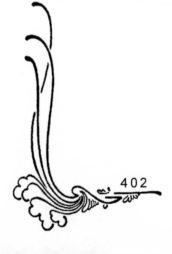

402

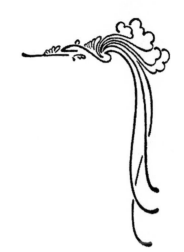

"Not I, Not I,
but the wind
that blows through me.
A fine wind is blowing
the new direction of time."

~ D.H. Lawrence

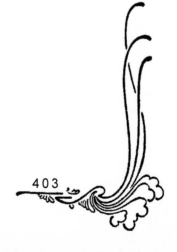

"Not only
is another world possible,
she is on her way.
On a quiet day,
I can hear her breathing."

~ Arundhati Roy

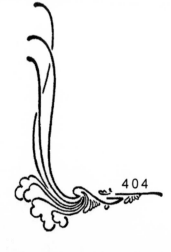

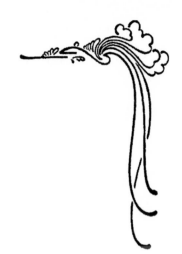

"Nothing great was ever achieved
without enthusiasm."

~ Ralph Waldo Emerson

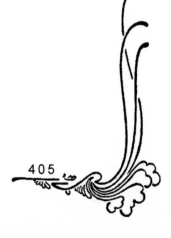

"*Nothing in life is to be feared.
It is only to be understood.*"

~ Marie Curie

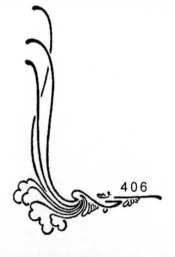

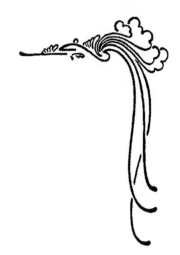

"Nothing in the world
can take the place of persistence."

~ Ray Kroc

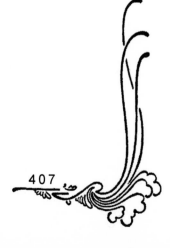

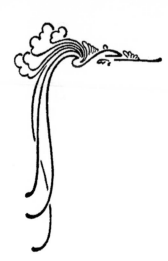

"Nothing is a waste of time
if you use the experience wisely."

~ Auguste Rodin

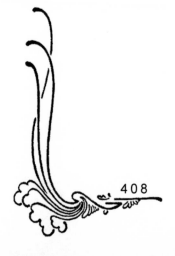

408

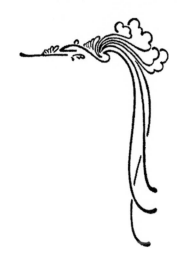

"Your heart and my heart
are very, very old friends."

~ Hafiz

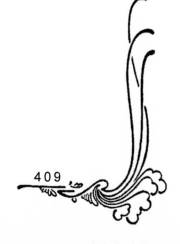

"*Nothing is more beautiful
than a believing heart.*"

~ Unknown

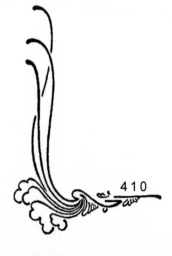

410

"Nothing will ever be attempted
if all possible objections
must first be overcome."

~ Samuel Johnson

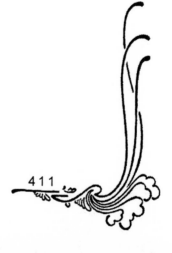

"*Observe your emotions,*
*be conscious of them.*
*The more you observe them,*
*the more you will learn*
*to manage them.*"

~ Unknown

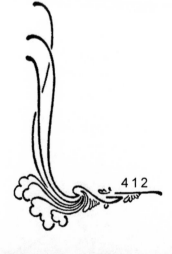

"*Obstacles
are those frightful things
you see when you take your eyes
off your goal.*"

~ Henry Ford

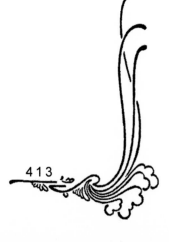

*"Once a problem is solved,
its simplicity is amazing."*

~ Unknown

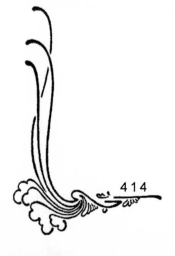

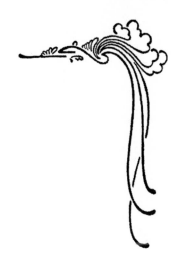

"*Once you choose hope,
anything is possible.*"

~ Christopher Reeve

415

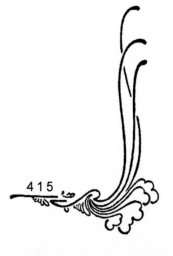

"*One can never consent to creep when one feels an impulse to soar.*"

~ Helen Keller

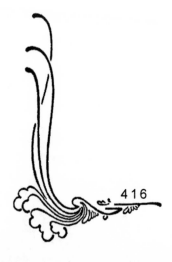

"One is left
with the horrible feeling
now that war settles nothing;
that to win a war
is as disastrous as to lose one."

~ Agatha Christie

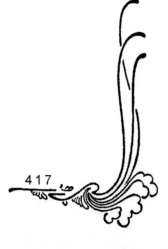

"*One may not reach
the dawn save by the path
of the night.*"

~ Kahlil Gibran

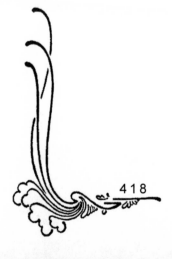

418

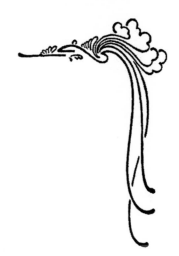

"*One must still have chaos in oneself to give birth to a dancing star.*"

~ Friedrich Nietzsche

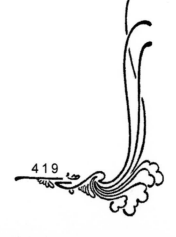

"One of life's biggest sins
is self-doubt."

~ Unknown

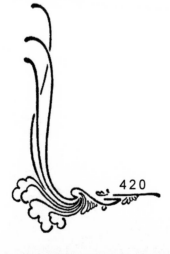

"One of
the most important things
a father can do
for his children
is to love their mother."

~ Theodore M. Hesburgh

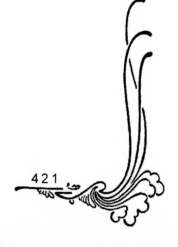

"*One secret of success in life is for a man to be ready for his opportunity when it comes.*"

~ Benjamin Disraeli

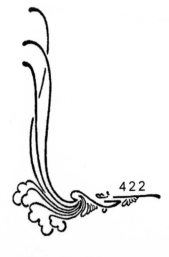

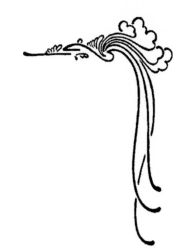

"One sees great things
from the valley;
only small things
from the peak."

~ G.K. Chesterton

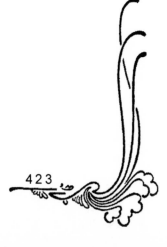

*"One today
is worth two tomorrows."*

~ Benjamin Franklin

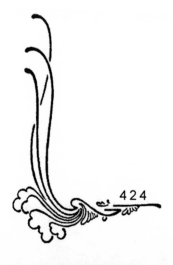

424

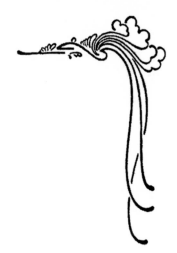

"One touch of nature
makes the whole world kin."

~ William Shakespeare

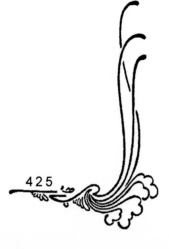

"*Only passions, great passions,
can elevate the soul
to great things.*"

~ Denis Diderot

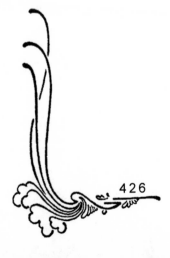

426

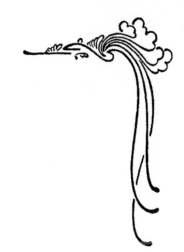

*"Only skydivers know why the birds sing."*

~ Saying on one of my old T-shirts

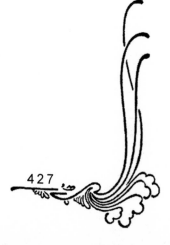

"Opportunity is missed
by most people because
it is dressed in overalls
and looks like work."

~ Thomas Edison

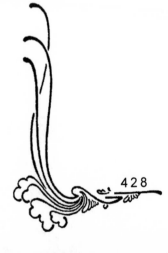

428

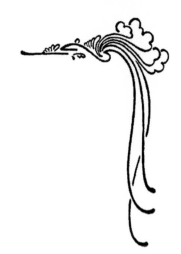

"*Optimism
is the foundation of courage.*"

~ Nicholas Murray Butler

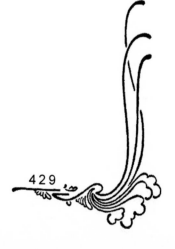

"*Other people
do not have to change
for us to experience
peace of mind.*"

~ Gerald Jampolsky

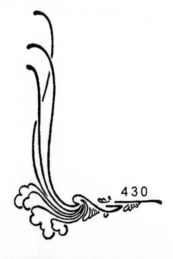

430

"*Our chief want
is someone who will inspire us
to be what we know
we could be.*"

~ Ralph Waldo Emerson

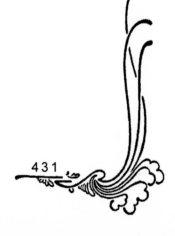

"*Our greatest glory
is not in never falling,
but in rising every time we fall.*"

~ Confucius

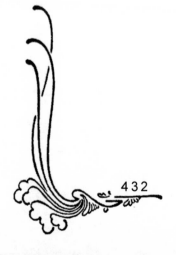

"*Our imagination
is the only limit
to what we can hope to have
in the future.*"

~ Charles F. Kettering

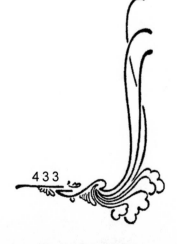

433

"*Our truest life
is when we are in dreams awake.*"

~ Henry David Thoreau

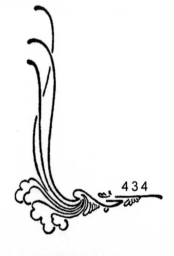

434

"Out beyond ideas
of wrongdoing and rightdoing,
there is a field.
I will meet you there."

~ Jalāl ad-Dīn Muhammad Balkhī "Rumi"

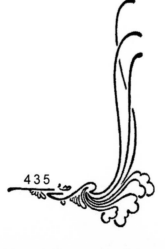

"*Patience
is also a form of action.*"

~ Auguste Rodin

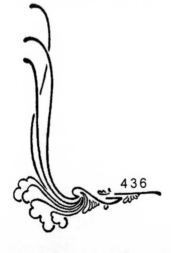

436

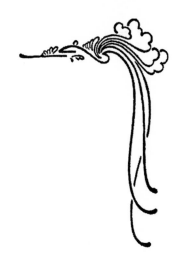

"*Peace has her victories
which are no less renowned
than war.*"

~ John Milton

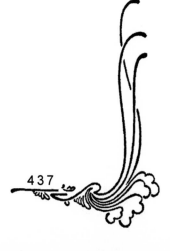

437

"*Peace is not achieved
by controlling nations,
but mastering our thoughts.*"

~ John Harricharan

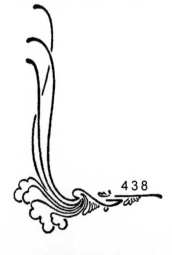

438

"Peace is not merely
a distant goal that we seek,
but a means by which
we arrive at that goal."

~ Martin Luther King, Jr.

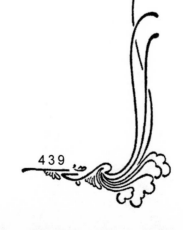

"*Peace is not something
you wish for;
it's something you make,
something you do,
something you are,
and
something you give away.*"

~ Robert Fulghum

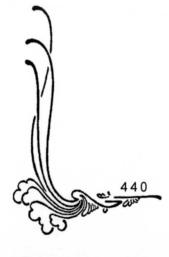

"*Peace of mind
is attained not
by ignoring problems,
but by solving them.*"

~ Raymond Hull

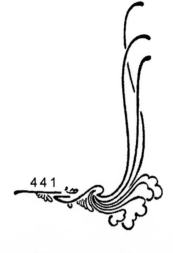

"Peace, like charity,
begins at home."

~ Franklin D. Roosevelt

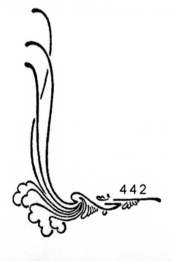

442

"Peace.
It doesn't mean to be in
a place with no noise,
trouble or hard work.
It means to be in the midst
of these things and still be
calm in your heart."

~ Unknown

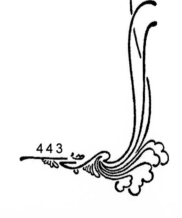

443

"*People are lonely
because they build walls
instead of bridges.*"

~ Joseph Newton

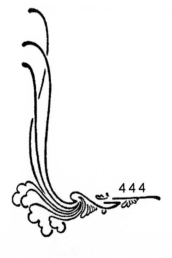

444

"People
even more than things
have to be restored, renewed,
revived, and reclaimed;
never throw out anyone."

~ Audrey Hepburn

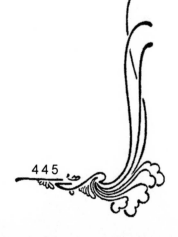

"*People who make no mistakes
lack boldness
and the spirit of adventure.
They are the brakes
on the wheels of progress.*"

~ Dale Turner

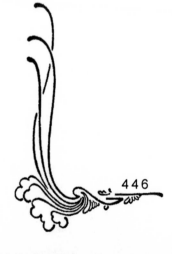

"People will forget
what you did,
but people will never forget
how you made them feel."

~ Maya Angelou

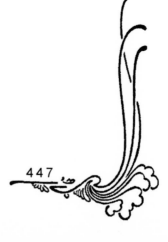

"*Person to person,
moment to moment,
as we love,
we change the world.*"

~ Samahria Lyte Kaufman

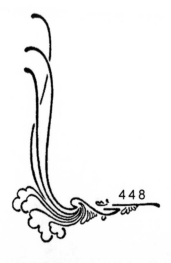

"We are the sun, the moon,
the stars, all there is.
Let us awaken to who we are
— infinitely open-ended."

~ Brent N. Hunter

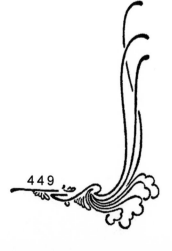

"*Practice
random acts of kindness
and senseless acts of beauty
every day.*"

~ Anne Herbert

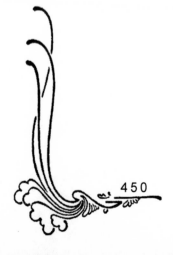

450

# About The Author

Brent Hunter is an author, social media pioneer, IT professional, and certified project manager who uses social media to help inspire and uplift in the spirit of international friendship.

Hunter graduated with a BS in Math and Computer Science from Clarkson University, an MS in Counseling and Human Relations from Villanova University, and the equivalent of an MS in Information Systems as a graduate of the fast-track General Electric Information Systems Management Program. Throughout his career, he has been involved in information technology and security for such notable companies as Blue Shield, Wells Fargo Bank, and General Electric. From 1994 to 2001, Mr. Hunter envisioned, produced and directed the web's first and largest all-inclusive, intentional World Community in cyberspace, The Park.

Hunter's first book, published in 1993, was titled *The Pieces of Our Puzzle* and provided a holistic synthesis of the world's major schools of psychology. Hunter's second book, *The Rainbow Bridge: Bridge to Inner Peace and to World Peace*, illuminates the common ground in the world's major wisdom traditions, also known as universal principles. *The Rainbow Bridge* is the recipient of the Living Now 2013 Bronze Medal for World Peace.

CPSIA information can be obtained at www.ICGtesting.com
Printed in the USA
LVOW05s1918041113

360011LV00001B/10/P